Redeemed

Redeemed

discovering identity after trauma

REBECCA KOLENDA

ISBN: 979-8-218-38515-6

This book is dedicated to

Jesus, the redeemer of my life's story
and
Jon, the love of my life.

*"Has the LORD redeemed you? Then speak out!
Tell others he has redeemed you from your enemies."*

Psalm 107:2 NLT

Preface

Today is the eighteenth day of November. The first snowfall of the season is swirling around outside my window. I'm sitting here at my window-view desk while this blank page glares at me from my computer screen. At this moment, I feel entirely humbled and in breathless awe of what I'm about to do. Only in the deepest, most secluded parts of my heart have I dared to dream of becoming an author and telling my story.

I first had the idea to become an author around nine years old. I'm not quite sure what piqued my interest in writing; however, I do recall several failed attempts to start a club with some of my neighborhood friends. That "club" inspired my first stories, simplistically titled *The B.F.F.E Club.*[1] Over the course of three years, I penned multiple short story adventures in *The B.F.F.E Club* saga. When I reached my pre-teen years, I realized how overtly juvenile they were, wincing in complete embarrassment. I decided that authoring was not for me, and

---

1. The Best Friends Forever Club. Clearly, I had not caught onto the concept of compound words and was unaware that "forever" is *not* two words.

I left it behind with the simplicities of childhood. However, a passion for writing remained with me. When I was sixteen years old, I wrote this journal entry:

"Looking at myself, I would not say that I am a writer, but looking back, I used to love writing my 'Best Friends Forever Club' stories. Writing down the way I feel and memories I have is something I enjoy and need to do sometimes. Sometimes, the only way to get out what I'm feeling is by writing."

Writing continues to be my haven, liberating me to disclose my innermost feelings, desires, and memories. It's a cathartic experience for my mind, body, and soul.

After experiencing decades of trauma that profoundly affected my core identity, I found myself entirely depleted and hopeless. Several months after my thirtieth birthday, I decided to prioritize my health and began a therapeutic journey toward soul recovery. Within these pages, I have found the energy to breathe again.

In preparation for writing this memoir, I relied on the memories, facts, and stories recorded in the versed journals of my past to reminisce about my life's journey—it's been one wild ride! I sat in the grief of loss, rejoiced in victories, wallowed in the void of unbearable pain, and walked along the hopeful road of promises yet to come—an extraordinary roller coaster of introspection. It's a beautiful, complex, unique illustration of my life.

Growing up, I doubted whether I had a testimony to share. Whenever I heard others tell their personal stories about salvation, they often included battles with addiction, physical abuse, suicidal thoughts, poverty, or religious conversion. I knew about Jesus' saving grace my entire life, and I didn't think that knowing God had really changed me—at least, not like it had in other people's lives. I envied these stories of rescue as a teenager, desperate for my own inspiring testimony. When I was seventeen years old, entering my senior year of high school, I journaled this entry:

"I know that God will help me through [school], and I hope I have a great testimony after it all!"

When I wrote that, I could not have imagined what God would do in my life. Now, remembering how passionate I was to discover who God created me to be, I can't help but sigh with utmost relief for God's faithfulness. It may have taken years for me to understand the soul-saving work God did in my life, but the beauty of His timing is that now, fifteen years after I had hoped for a testimony, I am publicly sharing my story of the Lord's saving grace. I no longer question the relevance of my salvation because I know that the significance of my testimony isn't in the dramatic rescue but in the act of being *redeemed*.

As I've reflected on my journey of redemption, I've discovered that being redeemed is more than just a spiritual transformation at the moment of salvation. I believe redemption is the unbelievable reality that God will also restore every hindrance welled within our souls. Redemption is not a one-time, happily-ever-after magical cure from suffering. It is a continuous opportunity for the Lord to bring *good* into our lives. As we grow in our faith and surrender our problems to God, He is faithful to redeem our difficulties and bring healing, restoration, and prosperity into our circumstances.

My sincerest hope is that my story is not only an example of God's faithfulness and unmerited grace but also a motivation, comfort, and inspiration for *you* to lead the life God has destined for you. I believe in 2 Corinthians 1:4 (NLT), which says, "He comforts us in all our troubles so that we can comfort others. When they are troubled, we will be able to give them the same comfort God has given us." My heartfelt prayer is that the stories and scriptures enclosed within these cherished pages cultivate hope in your own life and encourage you along your personal path of redemption, hardship, victory, and grace.

Here is where my testimony begins. This is how my life has been *redeemed*.

Chapter One

The Mantle

"Out of difficulties grow miracles…"

JEAN DE LA BRUYERE

Here I come! I was about three years old, frantically trying to find my mom in the early hours of the morning, my short brunette hair bobbing about as I rushed around the house. When I finally found her, I passionately declared, "Mommy! I get up and I play all day!" My mom laughed, tilted her head slightly to the side, her eyes filled with adoration toward her young daughter's zest for life, and simply said, "Yes, sweetheart, you do."

Whether it's the retelling of this memory throughout the years or my own recollection of the moment, I can still sense the joyfulness my three-year-old soul felt when I abandonedly expressed this revelation to my mom. I remember being taken aback by my mom's laughter, but then recognizing the care in her eyes and taking pride in my ability to make my mom *happy*.

Moments like these made me feel content. Seeing my mom's visible expression of love and joy, hearing an air of delight in her voice. Being a source of happiness for Mom was a privileged responsibility, one that I highly valued. Yet, I discovered that this honor was disguised as an oppressive mantle.[1] From a young age, I felt a subconscious responsibility to offset any unhappiness or misery in my parents' lives. Although figuratively wrapped in this cloak of atonement, I grasped onto its role with devotion. I pressured myself to be everyone's source of joy and began to define who I was by pleasing others. Inadvertently, I placed my very worth and identity on the mantle's expectation of perfection.

I was born on a dreary spring Wednesday morning in March 1992. Weighing in at seven pounds ten ounces with a purple complexion (due to the duration of labor) and an

---

1. A mantle is a cloak that symbolizes an important responsibility being handed down to an individual. In my life, the figurative mantle was the expectation I felt to be perfect and bring happiness to my family.

elongated, mostly bald head, I was "perfect from the beginning"—so says my mom. As a child, I never understood how wrinkly, purple, long-headed, bald *me* could be a representation of "perfect." But as an adult, I can now comprehend the significance of my birth story: I was this innocent, impeccable little person my parents were awarded amidst their troubles. I was their opportunity to make things right in life; my existence was their potential redemption.

I imagine that most parents have overwhelming emotions of infatuation toward their newborns. Nonetheless, I believe when children are born into trauma or are the outcome of a negative experience, the appreciation of their very existence can be viewed differently. The lives of those children can be seen as an opportunity for their parents to do better than their previous failures and past mistakes. It's quite a burden for a new human being, suddenly being expected to restore the fractured lives of their parents. Subconsciously, it's as if these parents predestine their children to be prized rewards. If they can produce a perfectly competent child, they can atone for their past shortcomings. Our existence—that is, of the babies born with the expectation of redemption—is a novelty, our lives presumably owned by our parents to shape and influence as they please. When we start to become our own persons, our parents are then surprised. Our emerging individuality shatters the illusion that we will fulfill their preconceived expectations.

From the beginning, my parents have always cherished me and genuinely desired the best for my life. Even so, I believe that the discovery of my mom's pregnancy kindled a fearful determination in my parents' hearts. My mom and dad had me in their early twenties, exactly ten months after their wedding and college graduation. When my mom reflects on her genesis of parenthood, she will often say, "I was just so young...", taking a methodical breath as if she's inhaling the freedom of the present moment and exhaling the negative energy from those challenging years long ago.

My parents wanted to live a good life, hopeful of releasing health, love, goodness, and Jesus into the world, especially for the sake of their new, impressionable baby girl. On my first birthday, my mom wrote this entry in my baby book:

> *"The world is a better place because you're in it! You bless so many people just by being you! You are just so amazing—the way you explore and examine everything and give love so freely... God has such a special plan for you!"*

Growing up, my parents expressed their sincere hope that I would have a better upbringing than they had both experienced as children. They wanted to raise a daughter who lived free from all the turmoil they had felt throughout their childhoods, and even though my birth was an unplanned surprise, they desperately tried to make their wishes my reality.

Christmas was a time when they fulfilled that desire the most. Many of my treasured childhood memories center around the Christmas season. For as long as I can remember, my parents invested special energy into our holiday traditions. Every Thanksgiving Day, while my mom busily cooked dinner, my dad would set up our artificial Christmas tree.[2] While Dad strung the multi-colored lights across each branch, I sat excitedly on the couch, watching the Macy's Thanksgiving Day Parade, patiently waiting to hang the ornaments together. As the smells of buttery mashed potatoes, salty corn-on-the-cob,

---

2. The era of living trees in our house had ended by the time I was six years old or so.

and roasted turkey wafted throughout the house, Dad and I (and my brothers once they were old enough) would take considerate time hanging each trinket, finding the perfect spot for every vintage, personalized, and sentimental ornament to be displayed along the delicate branches.

I was in the minority of American children who didn't believe in Santa Claus. My parents were honest about the magic of Santa and the historical facts of old Saint Nick. Even though I knew Santa wasn't real, I enjoyed visiting him at the mall and loved watching Christmas movies about the North Pole and Santa's workshop. I knew it was all a fun, magical, and pretend part of the holiday experience. My parents taught me that the significance of Christmas was about celebrating Jesus' birthday. They explained that the reason for gift-giving was because of the example God set when He gave us the ultimate gift—sending His son, Jesus, to live on earth and die for our sins. Believing in the truth of Christmas and experiencing a mix of traditions made celebrating the holiday extra special.

Most years, my family would spend a special night in December light-looking in different neighborhoods, admiring the creativity of each magically lit outdoor display. On other nights leading up to Christmas, we would gather in the living room under the multi-colored glow of our Christmas tree to read a special Advent story and then sing Christmas carols together. Our most epic tradition was baking a birthday cake for Jesus and eating it for breakfast on Christmas morning![3]

I absolutely cherished the Christmas season as a child. It was full of so much anticipation, intention, and magic. Even as a teenager, on the night of Christmas Eve, I'd feel excitement bouncing about in my stomach like the explosion of

---

3. This is a tradition I have yet to give up!

Pop Rock candies tingling my nerves as Christmas morning was about to dawn! I loved the routines of Christmas. It was the one day of the year my brothers and I were allowed to wake our parents up early. We'd crawl into their king-sized bed and snuggle up together while Dad read the Christmas story from Luke 2. Then, my brothers and I would creep downstairs to find the skirt of the Christmas tree entirely consumed by presents![4] As Christmas tunes played in the background, my brothers and I took turns opening our gifts, enthusiastically thanking our parents for each present. The magic of Christmas made me feel so *happy*. Our home was filled with joy; it was the best day of the year.

As I reflect on those fun-filled traditions, remembering the laughs my family shared and the excitement of the holiday season, I can still feel the tension and fear anchored within each memory. Throughout my upbringing, my parents constantly fought, becoming instantly irritated and impatient with each other. During holidays, their conflicts were kept to a minimum, but I still anticipated the friction. Sometimes peaceful moments lasted for a while, the calmness soothing my anxious spirit. Other times, the stress and strain from my parents' discord lingered for days on end.

My parents' constant arguing and hurtful language influenced the dysfunction of our home life. Even though they would apologize to my brothers and me about their fighting, that didn't stop it from happening again (and again). To cope with the instability, it seemed like my family tried to mask the problem, not dealing with the heart of the issue and not telling anyone what *really* happened in our household. Such an

---

4. Mom waited until Christmas Eve to wrap our gifts and put them under the tree for the morning reveal.

unstable environment reinforced my obligation to the mantle for perfect atonement, intensified my fear of conflict, and negatively impacted my understanding of love, communication, and boundaries. Although their loud arguments were saved for the privacy of our home, I internally felt the stress of my parents' arguments even when they suppressed their frustrations. Their continuous strife caused emotional turmoil within my young soul.

The struggles that my parents have faced are stories only they are privileged to tell. However, as our lives have obviously shared mutual experiences, it is my prerogative to tell my story from my own point of view. My parents' perspectives about my upbringing may differ from my memories and opinions, but that does not negate the truth of my interpretations.

From the depths of my heart, I believe that my parents had no intention of placing the responsibility of redemption on my shoulders. I assume that my existence ignited their determination to do their best in life, an obligation solely for *them* to bear. However, their desire for better transferred emotionally to my subconscious, becoming a burden for approval that I clung to *invincibly*.

⊷—• •—⊶

As a young child, I strove to keep the peace between my parents and faithfully resolved to be their source of happiness, especially for my mom. Numerous times throughout my childhood, my dad would talk about their lives before my birth, specifically the fact that my mom had other aspirations in life that didn't include parenthood. Although the discussion was often phrased like, "Mom didn't want to be a mommy until she had you, and now she's so happy you were born! Mommy loves you so much!", all that echoed in my mind was:

"Mom didn't want to be a mommy, but she had you…"

"Mom wanted a career, but she had you…"

"Mom wanted…but you."

These words blared like a foghorn in my ears, reminding me of the disappointment of my existence. In those moments, my self-esteem dipped so low that I felt like my life was of no worth at all. Even though my mom assured me of her love and expressed her appreciation for my existence, it took my heart years to look past the "but…" I had fabricated. My life's value was never dependent on her unplanned pregnancy.

Sometimes during my parents' incessant fighting, I would lay in my twin-sized bed with its nineties *Winnie the Pooh* comforter set, wiping my tears on the edge of my pillowcase, pondering their argument, grieved by the strife between them. Eventually, I concluded that it was all my fault. If I hadn't been born, my parents would have gotten a divorce. If I didn't exist, my parents would be happy. I assumed that I was the cause of their unhappiness, and that realization tore my heart in two. My self-worth was attached to my parents' contentment. My life's value meant nothing if I wasn't atoning for their happiness, and I was disappointed with myself for causing such a burden in their lives.

This idea that my existence negatively impacted my parents' marriage was one that I believed and grieved over into adulthood. Now that I've begun to process my past trauma, I realize that it was a *very* false assumption. Marriages and relationships are much more complicated than a young child can comprehend. My existence was never the root cause of my parents' miserable marriage.

However, the pressure from the mantle's expectation of redemption remained on my shoulders. Because my parents desired such improvement and betterment for my life due to their own difficult childhoods, I believed that I bore the obligation to be their good, perfect, and pleasing reward.

As I grew up, I started suppressing my personal desires and placing everyone else's feelings above my own, not valuing my own ambitions unless they were approved by someone else. I felt great satisfaction knowing that my selfless actions gratified others' desires, and their expression of enjoyment made me feel valued, loved, and accepted. I began to find my identity, the very worth of my life's existence, in the perfectionist efforts of the mantle's demands.

When my eleventh birthday was approaching, I discovered that Christian singer Steven Curtis Chapman was coming to our city for his concert tour *on my birthday*! It was the perfect present to ask for; I was a huge fan! But just as quickly as the excitement came, I extinguished its delight. I knew that our family finances were tight, and the concert tickets weren't cheap. However, when my parents asked if I'd like to attend the concert, I told them I didn't want to go. My due diligence toward the mantle would not permit me to accept such a selfish reward, even if it was my birthday. Money greatly strained my parents' marriage, and I didn't want to cause another burden. At eleven years old, I chose not to attend the concert—one that would've been a dream to go to—to savor an ounce of contentment between my parents.

My personality as a little girl was one of joy, enthusiasm, and love. My dad described my temperament as *sanguine* because of my cheerful and energetic demeanor. Most of my childhood days were spent in imaginative play. Whether it was with my baby dolls, toy cars, or stuffed animals, I imagined a variety of drama and adventure for my toy companions. From using my bed as a Pioneer wagon like Laura Ingalls' family drove, to transforming our couch into a shipwrecked island from *The Swiss Family Robinson*, or sliding across the cold, cement basement floor in my socks and pretending it was an ice rink for Olympic skaters, I had a vivid imagination during playtime. Since I was an only child until the age of seven (and homeschooled), I spent much of my time alone with my imagination. I loved going outside to compose new scenarios for my play, where I would hide behind trees from criminals or operate my bike as a vehicle in an amateur drag race. I was always thinking, constantly devising new plot schemes to implement into my play routines.[5] Of course, I was the leading actress in every scene and played every part my toys couldn't portray. This active, whimsical, pretend play was my outlet to express myself and subconsciously escape from the negativity surrounding my life.

The one environment I always felt safe within was church. Throughout my childhood, my family constantly attended church every Sunday morning and frequented Wednesday night services. Each time I entered the foyer as a young girl, I felt a peacefulness saturate my soul as if I could sense the protective love of Christ within the mortar walls. The church building wasn't anything special, nothing like the exquisite

---

5. I think that's one reason that my brain never shuts off now as an adult. I conditioned myself at a young age to keep my mind running!

structures throughout Europe with their rich religious history and ornate features. But the enjoyment of experiencing life inside such an ordinary building was captivating. I loved attending children's church, worshiping with the music videos, learning Bible lessons, watching puppet shows, and receiving a "cowboy buck" whenever I brought my Bible or memorized the weekly memory verse.[6] When I was about four years old, I desperately wished that I could live at church forever, a desire I now assume was influenced by my home life. Being at church was a weekly opportunity for me to physically leave the overbearing tension and allow my soul a moment to breathe. I gravitated toward the liberation created by the presence of God's lovingkindness in everything I experienced at church.

As devoted Christ-followers, my parents put the pursuit of a relationship with Jesus at the top of my life's agenda. My parents both grew up with the knowledge of Christianity, but it wasn't until college that they decided to dedicate their lives to Jesus and begin an exclusive relationship with Him. When they became parents, they were committed to upholding the biblical wisdom in Proverbs 22:6 (NKJV), which says, "Train up a child in the way he should go, And when he is old he will not depart from it."

My parents tried to accomplish this training by instilling wholesome values into my life through listening to praise and worship music, watching Christian-centered TV shows,[7] reading Bible stories before bedtime, and memorizing scripture. When I was a toddler, my parents taught me sayings like, "Praise Jesus!" and "Hallelujah!", and whenever I heard

---

6. Going shopping in the general store when you collected enough "bucks" was a Sunday morning highlight!
7. *The Donut Man*, *McGee & Me*, *Bibleman*, *Superbook*, and *The Story Keepers* were a few of my childhood favorites.

worship music, I learned to lift my tiny hands toward heaven and sway back and forth to the sedated tempo. My parents' sincerest desire was for the consistency of these habits to plant a seed of faith in my heart and for my life to become rooted in a personal relationship with Christ. I believe the Lord honored their desire because no matter what trials I've faced, I've always returned to my faith in Jesus—my Lord, Savior, and *Redeemer*.

My parents always prayed over my life, trusting the Lord to bring salvation, love, and happiness into my future. On my first birthday, my dad recorded this entry in my baby book:

> *"Jesus has made you so special…Just the way you smile and laugh brings so much joy to everyone around you…I do know that God has a very special plan for your life. He loves you so much and will always take care of you."*

And when I was three years old, my mom wrote this entry in my baby book:

> *"You love to talk about God and read your Bible…you tell us you have Jesus in your heart, and you understand God made everything."*

Believing in Jesus always felt *right*. Knowing that God created me, destined me for a special purpose, and cared about me brought comfort to my soul. As a young girl, I absorbed all I could learn from Bible stories, children's church services, and the positive message of Jesus' gift of salvation. I began to develop a close connection to the Lord and desired to live according to His will. In the innocence of my faith, I believe Jesus took hold of my heart and secured my life into His abounding mercy, love, and grace. I may not have understood the concept of my identity yet, but I knew that acceptance could be found in the security of my relationship with Jesus.

⬦⸻ ⸻⬦

Learning how to be a Christian from my parents' example was a bit overwhelming. My family strove to live a virtuous lifestyle (despite the regular chaos in our home); the religious expectations of obedience, godliness, and purity intensified the pressure of the mantle's perfect standard for my life.

As a kid, I always knew my family was different because we believed in Jesus and (I assumed) most other people didn't—or at least they weren't *real* Christians like us. My secular neighborhood friends knew I was a Christian and that I wasn't allowed to be influenced by certain worldly habits. When I was around eight years old, a neighborhood friend told me about a swear word. My friend avoided condemnation by spelling it creatively: *"H-E-Double Hockey Sticks."* I decided to say it out loud—Hell. I didn't realize it was a bad word because I previously had learned that it was the place where Satan lived. After I said it—*Hell*—my friend gasped in astonishment, astounded that the Christian girl just said a swear word! I felt embarrassed and confused having just made a terrible mistake, terrified of the consequences to come. Fortunately, I didn't get in trouble because Hell *is* a real place, but I was told never to say it again.

When I was young, my parents rarely allowed me to play at my neighborhood friends' houses, always requiring me to invite them to our home or play outside together instead. On a once-in-a-blue-moon day when I was about ten years old, I went to a friend's house to play Barbies. I remember her mom carrying on a loud conversation with someone else in the house, and as she exclaimed an obscene word aloud, my friend frantically called down to her mom and cautiously reminded her, "You can't say that around Becca!" Although my friend was trying to be caring toward my religious upbringing, I felt embarrassed that people were expected to act differently around me. I know that protection from such crude language is mentally healthy for a child, but the fact that people felt like they couldn't be themselves around me was humiliating to my insecure self. At the same time, anxiety bubbled up from my gut as I worried about the terrible experience I just had. I feared that overhearing something bad or observing something ungodly, such as any obscene word or sinful habit, would enter my spirit and its detrimental, second-hand effects haunted my every breath.

The proverbial principle to "*see no evil, hear no evil, speak no evil*" ran through my veins as I built beliefs from these secular experiences, judging every interaction with the religious lens of perfectionism. As a child, I was determined not to let anything bad make me unworthy of holy atonement, and I affixed my life's value to that objective. Although I didn't understand my fear of moral approval, the seed of anxiety was planted, and its tentacle-like roots spread throughout the soil of my heart. Doing something wrong (even making a simple mistake) or acting badly (in any unbiblical manner) was unacceptable in my mind. The expectation to always do the right thing was overwhelming, giving shame and guilt control of my thoughts.

The undergrowth of anxiousness remained nurtured throughout my childhood, adolescence, and into adulthood. Even as I've presently worked to remove the deep-seated roots of perfectionism, cutting off each untangled sprig from the well-nourished remnant of anxiety, I still struggle to live completely free. One practice that has helped me pull up these weeds of apprehension is learning from Scripture. Looking at my worries through a lens of biblical wisdom has given me the insight to understand what I should believe about living a Christian lifestyle.

I've always known that sin influences our worthiness in being pure and innocent before God. Yet, realizing that I'll never amount to God's standard of righteousness discouraged the perfectionist in me. How could I receive salvation, something I could never earn, and still not meet God's expectation of holiness? In my despair, I found this scripture in Ecclesiastes 7:20 (NLT): "Not a single person on earth is always good and never sins." The reality of this verse helped me understand it's not about my ability to reach the Lord's glorious standard; it's about His grace to meet me where I am regardless of my inabilities. Realizing that God already knows I'm not going to be perfect and that I won't always do the right thing (despite my best intentions) has brought peace to my soul.

As I processed Scripture, I realized Christians are not meant to be superhumans. We are simply flawed individuals called to live righteous lives through the forgiveness of our sins. We will never live up to perfect standards, but we can live grace-filled lives of righteousness. By accepting my humanness, I've begun to understand that I don't have to worry about my imperfect actions. Although there are no excuses for outright disobedience, there is mercy in having every mistake forgiven. No matter what mistakes we make, we can freely receive God's forgiveness through repentance. Every sinful deed is of equal value, and each repentant action is worthy of utmost forgiveness by our loving Savior.

—◆——— ———◆—

One Christmas when I was about nine years old, we traveled to visit family for the holiday (an unusual occurrence for us). We went to a family member's house for a festive gathering of fellowship, food, and fun. Before dinner, the family member said a prayer of blessing over the meal, every eye closed and head bowed as he led us in a petition of grace. During his prayer, my eyelids refused to close as I stared in amazement at the sight before me. As the family member prayed, I noticed he was holding a bottle of beer in his fist.

A. Bottle. Of. Beer.

I thought, *How ghastly for someone to attempt petitioning the Lord while they're drinking!*[8] To indulge in alcohol—period—was an unforgivable sin according to the lessons I was learning from my parents' disapproval of the habit.

When I was a child and saw someone behaving in (what I believed to be) an unchristian-like manner, I assumed that the person couldn't possibly love Jesus because I knew a true Christian made no mistakes in leading a life of moral perfection to please God. Whether by observation or direct discipline, I learned to judge the actions of others to determine their religious legitimacy.[9] I knew the virtuous Ten Commandments that Christians are expected to follow—which I believed my parents diligently obeyed regardless of the conflicts brewing in our home. I believed that we were striving along the righteous path of living while so many others were distracted by the temptations of worldly sins.

As an adult, I've realized the hypocritical habit I acquired by judging others. In Matthew 7:3, Jesus specifically warns us

---

8. My thought probably wasn't that sophisticated, but you get the picture.
9. A very wrong approach to the command found in Matthew 7:1, which says, "Do not judge, or you too will be judged…"

of this offense, saying, "'Why do you look at the speck of saw-dust in your brother's eye and pay no attention to the plank in your own eye?'" Although people don't go walking around with planks of wood protruding from their eyeballs, each person on this planet has their own battles, beliefs, situations, and habits that either positively or negatively affect their lives. Even when I disagree with someone else's life choices, I should not place them into a predetermined "bad" category nor judge their intentions. Someone might make bad decisions, but that doesn't make them a bad person, especially not by my imperfect standards.

I've also learned that everyone has the privilege to decide what is right or wrong for the health of their physical lives and spiritual souls. If I'm tempted or negatively impacted by someone else's choices, I have the right to abstain from those uncomfortable situations, but I don't have the authority to judge them and ridicule their habits. In John 13:34, Jesus Himself says, "A new command I give you: Love one another. As I have loved you, so you must love one another." There is no love in critical judgments. Just because someone does not practice the same ideals that I value doesn't permit me to judge their decisions. If I want to live a life of righteousness, I must love others despite their imperfect humanness, just like Jesus did.

Throughout my childhood, I never questioned my parents' religious beliefs or the moral lessons I was learning from them. I held their authority in high esteem, the mantle's expectations reminding me of my purpose to adhere and obey. I was afraid of not appeasing my parents and worked hard to gain their approval through my upright choices.[10] In everything I did, the mantle maliciously conferred with my subconscious, fearfully

---

10. I also feared upsetting God, which would disappoint my parents, too.

reminding me of my responsibility to make atonement for my family's happiness.

As a child, I was afraid of punishment, nervous about making any false moves because I felt the need to be *perfect*. But as I grew up, I finally began to understand that it isn't *me* who is supposed to be perfect, it's *Jesus*—He was, is, and forever will be *perfect*. The worth that I place in my efforts will never equal the value of Christ's love for me. In His perfect love, every fear is extinguished and every anxiety is abolished. First Peter 5:7 (NLT) commands: "Give all your worries and cares to God, for he cares about you." As I choose to believe that the Lord genuinely cares about me, I learn to trust Him with the worries of my heart, offering them to Jesus in prayer and receiving peace and compassion in return. Giving my brokenness to God and moving past my hurt isn't an instantaneous fix; it's a consistent act of humility and repentance. As I continue to seek Jesus' loving care, He is faithful to bring solace, healing, and restoration to whatever I am willing to give to Him.

Somewhere along my journey of healing, growing, and becoming, I've discovered that words matter. I believe that the things spoken into your life have immense significance. Growing up with two younger brothers (seven and ten years my junior), I watched the beloved children's show *Veggie Tales* far past my childhood prime. At the end of every episode, Bob the Tomato and Larry the Cucumber warmly declare that *"God made you special, and He loves you very much!"* The truth of this simplistic quote made by two animated vegetables taught me the value I have in the Lord's loving care, and it is a phrase that

I continue to proclaim throughout my life and into the lives of others. Believing that God sincerely loves you and created you to be the unique, wonderful person that you are is a reprieve so liberating that it can entirely transform your life for the better. In the darkest moments of overwhelming pain, amidst misery and agony, when I regretted my life as a young girl and wished I'd never been born, I found great comfort in knowing God made me on purpose and that He loved me no matter what.

I'll never forget the moment I asked Jesus into my heart and chose to become a Christian; it's an experience forever imprinted in my mind. I was about three years old, curled up on the blue couch in our dimly lit living room. It was early in the morning, and I was watching the children's program *The Gospel Bill Show* via our box television screen. At the end of every episode, Gospel Bill led the viewers in a simple prayer of salvation. On this particular morning, I repeated the prayer and asked Christ into my heart. Afterward, I didn't feel anything different inside—no rustling, whishing, pattering, or pounding, as I assumed would happen when someone came to live inside your heart. I prayed the salvation prayer a few more times, just to make sure Jesus did come to live with me. Eventually, I guessed that He must've moved in more quietly than I had expected!

This was the most significant decision I've ever made. I believe that when my three-year-old self made that choice, God took the invitation and established His permanent residence in my life, just as Ephesians 3:17 (NLT) says: "Then Christ will make his home in your hearts as you trust in him. Your roots will grow down into God's love and keep you strong."

As God made His home in my heart, I believe His objective was to preserve my life by hemming me into the safety of His love, mercy, and faithfulness. Through my faith in Christ, I've developed the strength to persevere amidst hard circumstances and found the courage to heal and grow along my adulthood journey. Although I've suffered negative effects from my dysfunctional childhood, I have undeniably seen the Lord's protective hand throughout my life. There's no other rhyme or reason for the breakthroughs, blessings, and victories I've reaped except for the abundant goodness of the Lord. My relationship with Christ has been a constant anchor for my soul to rely on, giving me the freedom to discover who I am and understand who God created me to become.

In Galatians 1:15 (NLT), the Apostle Paul says, "But even before I was born, God chose me and called me by his marvelous grace..." Although Paul is referring to his personal life and unique destiny, I believe this wisdom applies to every human life. The truth of this verse is mesmerizing—the idea that God chose me before my life even began, that He called me by grace for a specific purpose. In the sincerity of this scripture, I see the unbelievable love of God. He didn't need me to prove myself worthy of love or purpose; He had already chosen to love me and even designed a specific purpose for my life. To love someone unconditionally is a choice, and the Lord's love surpasses all my expectations.

Throughout my life, I've struggled to accept myself and, therefore, the love of Christ. I grew up learning and believing what the Bible says about God's unconditional love, but because of the pressure from the mantle and the damaging effects of my childhood trauma, I didn't think I was worthy of being truly loved. I felt safe and welcomed in my relationship with Christ, but I believed that His love toward me should be limited due to my flaws and failures. In the vulnerability of my doubts, I had to learn that my purpose was more than being a redemptive atonement. God created me not because of what my efforts could achieve but because He loved me. By recognizing my worth outside of the mantle's expectations, I began to release myself into the compassionate arms of my Savior. Knowing that God loves me despite my imperfections has brought freedom to my soul. Undoubtedly, the mantle's lasting impact reminds me of my inadequacy, but I now know I am worthy of God's love. No matter what I may believe about myself, through His unfailing love, I am *enough*.

Although I've learned to accept God's love, I've wrestled with the promise found in Jeremiah 29:11 (NLT), which says, "'For I know the plans I have for you,' says the Lord. 'They are plans for good and not for disaster, to give you a future and a hope.'" Throughout the years, I've questioned God in different ways about this scripture:

If His plans are for good, why wasn't my family happy?

If He knew the plan, why was I going through disaster?

If He planned to give me a future and a hope, why was the damage of my past affecting my life?

Honestly, it's difficult to find absolute answers to these questions. I believe that due to the sinful world we live in, not every hardship can be explained. Yet, I know that God does have *good* plans for everything He creates. And even in the doubt and confusion of His plans, I've witnessed the Lord's faithfulness. The one thing that has brought the most reassurance to my questions has been the reality of God's unwavering love. Psalm 138:8 (NLT) states, "The LORD will work out his plans for my life—for your faithful love, O LORD, endures forever." In this truth, I can release my doubts, worries, confusion, and frustration. I can trust that through His faithful love, His plans for my life *will* work out. It might not be in my timing or what I expect, but when I choose to rest in the Lord's promises, believing that God's Word will **not** return to Him empty, He will accomplish what He has desired, and it will achieve the purpose for which He intended it.[11]

There is no doubt in my mind that God orchestrates every detail of our lives. He takes every good choice, every mistake, every positive experience, and every tragedy, and twirls them together to create a beautiful purpose in our lives. And it is in that purpose that we find who we truly are—loved, chosen, accepted, and *redeemed*.

These lessons about God's love and purpose have taken a while for me to understand completely. A lot of what we learn through Scripture takes time to accept, especially when it involves something we've struggled to believe. There are days when I still question God's faithfulness, yet I believe His promises are true, and I choose to remember the good and not dwell on the unknown. Studying God's Word has taught me the life-changing power of Scripture that can encourage us in our finest hour, direct us amid obscurity, and comfort us in the darkest valley. No matter where we are in life, God is always there, and even when we don't understand it, He will see us through.

---

11. Isaiah 55:11.

Chapter Two

The Trauma

"There is no situation so chaotic that God cannot...create something that is surpassingly good. He did it at the creation. He did it at the cross. He is doing it today."

HANDLEY C. G. MOULE

*I*t's the most wonderful time of the year. As the story goes, it was a wintry night in December 1988 when my parents watched the beloved holiday classic *Rudolph the Red-Nosed Reindeer.* As Clarice tells Rudolph she thinks he's cute and Rudolph enthusiastically leaps into the air with abounding joy across the television screen, my dad turned excitedly toward my mom and asked: "Will you go steady with me?"

My parents met in their sophomore year at Penn State University. Although they were pursuing different majors—my mom seeking a degree in psychology and my dad aspiring toward a degree in criminal justice—both programs required Speech Composition 100, and thus destiny presented itself. Their professor had assigned seats alphabetically by last name; as fate would have it, both my parents' last names began with *M.* The following summer, my dad asked my mom the next inevitable question: "Will you marry me?"

My parents were married on a beautiful, sunny spring day in May 1991, just two weeks after their commencement from Penn State. With their hard-earned college degrees in hand and wedding rings on their fingers, their future was a blank canvas ready for life's colorful brushstrokes to create an award-winning masterpiece of novelty, love, and success. Exactly ten months later, my parents began the unexpected adventure of *parenthood.*

Telling my story unavoidably includes difficult, heart-breaking, and shameful details. I'm not here to disclose secrets of my parents' past nor recall my own experiences with accu-satory intentions. I simply want to share my truth honestly. Despite our family dysfunction, I believe my parents always had good intentions of creating a nurturing upbringing for my brothers and me. Seemingly, the hindrance of strife, fear, hurt, and disappointment prevented my parents from creating the redemptive life they had hoped to attain.

⊷——•—•—⊶

I cannot recall exactly how fights began between my parents, but when they were in conflict, I knew it. Whether the silence in the atmosphere grew dense, their attitudes became stiff and passive, or I heard their disputes flaring up, I knew an aggressive exchange was about to happen.

One of my earliest memories is listening to my parents fighting. I was three years old, and it was bedtime. As I laid on my twin-size bed, staring at the yellow, green, and purple poster of Barney the Dinosaur hanging on my bedroom door, I listened to the shouts of frustration between my parents as they yelled at each other throughout the house. When my mom finally came into my room to say goodnight, I told her, "Mommy, you should say sorry to Daddy, and Daddy should say sorry to Mommy."

I'm sure my mom took a deep breath, attempting not to roll her eyes in irritation, before shouting, "Sorry!" down the hallway. I recall my dad reciprocating with a shout of "Sorry," and I joyfully hugged my mom, grinning from ear to ear, as I enthusiastically said, "Now everything's all better!" Oh, what innocent faith I had in assisting my parents' happiness! The pride I felt in persuading my parents' apology made my spirit soar. In those moments, my inner self felt whole. I had caused something good to happen between my parents, influencing the mantle's power in my life.

As a young child, I couldn't recognize the source of stress—nor identify that I was under stress at all. However, I inadvertently experienced excessive amounts of anxiety whenever my parents fought. Even as I grew older, my parents' lack of contentment affected the stability of my emotional well-being. At eleven years old, I wrote this simple entry: *"Today my mom and dad are mad. Lord, please have it stop!"* and at sixteen years old, I journaled, *"...my parents had been going through a hard time, which meant I was too."* Growing up, all I wanted was for my parents to be happy, for joy and peace to consume our home. My naïve self presumed I could control this desire for happiness, so I draped the mantle proudly over my shoulders, becoming more accustomed to my role of atonement.

As a child, you're unaware of how the life lessons you're learning, habits you're forming, and beliefs you're trusting influence the development of the person you're becoming. It isn't until you're an adult and must face these insecure, vulnerable, anxious, and shameful biases that you recognize the effects of those past inaccuracies. Observing my parents' frequent fights hindered my understanding of how to act and be treated as a respected and loved human being. Instead of believing I deserved to be cherished, I learned (by their actions toward each other) that I should be ridiculed for my shortcomings and shamed for my downfalls. Subconsciously, I began to believe that this was how people treated each other, and I internalized these habits as acceptable and normal.

When I was born, I held the highest honor of being my family's "first"—first child, first niece, first grandchild, etc. Although every extended family member was excited about my existence, my GG was especially proud to be my Great-Grandma.

Through the years, our relationship bloomed into a special bond filled with genuine love, devotion, and care. Whenever we visited each other, we'd spend hours reading, playing, laughing, and talking. The love and pride she expressed during our time together always made me feel special.

Our favorite pastime was playing Barbies—GG portrayed the handsome and intellectual Ken dolls, and I personified the beautiful and impressionable Barbie dolls. Sometimes, I wanted Ken and Barbie to have an argument where they would yell at one another, apologize, and live happily ever after. GG would become rather disgruntled by this request, firmly telling me, "Rebecca, I will not play that way." One day, I must've gotten a bit feisty with her about it because I remember GG giving me her usual statement, and then she walked out on our playtime together.

I never could understand why GG didn't want to act out this scenario; wasn't this how things worked in real life anyway? It wasn't until college that one of my best friends asked, "Did you want to play that way because of the fighting you saw between your parents?"

Mind. Blown.

I had never realized that the scenarios I expressed through play were often related to the circumstances I was experiencing in my own life. This was an epiphany for the ages.

Back in 2018, my husband, Jon, and I were watching the movie *I Can Only Imagine,* inspired by the composition of the popular song by MercyMe. A portion of the movie depicts the songwriter's past childhood. One segment reveals a fierce verbal conflict between his parents. In the scene, his parents are shouting at one another like two lions in a roaring match while their son listens deadpan, lying in his bed with headphones on to drown out the noise of his parents' screams. As I watched this incident escalate on-screen, I recalled those undoubtedly identical moments I had witnessed between my parents. I could physically feel the fear and agony emanating from each actor's emotional performance because those sensations are *real*; they have flowed through my veins for many years.

When the scene ended, I paused the movie and asked Jon if his parents had ever fought that way when he was young (even though I already knew the answer). When he said "no," it was like an unforeseen slap in the face. I knew that my in-laws built a healthy marriage and displayed devoted love toward each other which influenced the unconditional way Jon has always loved me. However, in this moment, his response jostled the truth I longed to conceal—*I was from a broken family.*

It's not that this moment was an epiphany; I knew years ago that I came from trauma and dysfunction. It was simply a reminder of the negative environment I grew up in and the damaging circumstances that children from healthy, wholesome homes never experience. I was reminded of the hardships of my childhood and the significant barriers I've had to face throughout adulthood to achieve a smidgen of healing, success, and wholeness.

From my perspective, the biggest issue that affected my parents' marriage, and consequently my upbringing, was their lack of conflict resolution. Whenever disputes arose between them, their immediate defense seemed to be harsh accusations shouted throughout our home. I remember one fight they had when

I was about twelve years old. Mom and Dad had begun arguing in the kitchen, attempting to keep their fight hushed and muffled to protect the innocent ears of my brothers who were running around the house. Then, just like the anticipated explosion of a ticking time bomb, my parents' argument erupted in belligerent screams and aggressive sobs. Mom tried to escape upstairs for seclusion, but Dad was following right behind her. As Dad chased Mom up the steps, he yelled crude things at her until she finally reached their bedroom and slammed the door shut. Even still, Dad continued shouting horrible comments at the locked door as Mom wept in anguish behind it.

Regrettably, fights like these were all too common in our home. It was a miserable and terrifying scene to watch and hear as a child—the constant screaming, endless crying, malicious accusations, and aggressive pursuit around the house. I can't imagine how high my adrenaline and cortisol levels were while watching and listening to these episodes. It felt like pure chaos in my young mind, like a constant swirl of disarray with no handle to grasp onto in hopes of stability. As I grew older, I understood every disparaging word between my parents, every hurtful comment and shameful criticism used strategically to devastate the other. However, when I was little, the mayhem of their banter sounded like utter nonsense, foreign jargon lashing out in blaring tones from my parents' lips. I didn't understand the significance of what was shouted across the room, but I recognized the outrage in every syllable. I cannot recall the duration of their fights, but the agony it caused made it feel like their disputes lasted for hours on end; being in the midst of such intense and hurtful screaming was exhausting.

Once when I was about ten years old, we were on our way to Wednesday night church in the middle of a bitter dispute between my parents. As they continued their argument during our half-hour drive, the angst inside my gut grew, my heart beating as if it were racing in the Kentucky Derby. I felt scared being around the heat of their conflicts, feeling the tension between them boil, and I was nervous about what would happen once we arrived at church.

Although my parents never explicitly said not to tell anyone about the dysfunction in our household, I knew that people weren't supposed to know about my parents' constant fighting. Their conflicts were usually kept for the secrecy of our home, and I didn't know how they were going to cover up this quarrel before we got to church. However, my worries were soon dismissed because as Dad parked the car, my parents abruptly paused their argument, all of us walking into church together with bogus smiles on our faces and sorrow entrapped within our hearts. Although I'm sure friends and family knew about the discord in my parents' marriage, I don't believe anyone understood the reality of it all, how it was damaging not just their relationship but their children's lives, too.

The frequency of my parents' fighting varied depending on life's circumstances, but the reliability that conflict would reoccur was inevitable. One afternoon when I was about eight years old, I was sitting on the porch with my neighborhood friends when suddenly, I heard familiar shouting drifting into the atmosphere. Instantly, embarrassment crept up from my gut as my cheeks became pink, the mortifying realization that my friends were listening to the outraged voices coming from our kitchen window. I rushed inside the house and pleaded for my parents to stop fighting. Although my mom closed the kitchen window, I'm confident their argument didn't end there.

Many of their fights included my plea to end the controversy peacefully; sometimes it worked, sometimes it didn't. I
can recall several times when their conflicts were so intense
that Mom would leave the house, desperate to release her
emotional turmoil. I was frightened whenever she left, wondering when she would return, considering whether happiness
was even possible. A rush of relief washed over me every time
Mom came back and the tension died down.

Moments of peace and calm were often overshadowed by
the weight of my parents' verbal abuse. Even when life seemed
okay, I always anticipated the next eruption. The prospect of
possible outrage hung in the air like a dense fog—sometimes,
it stayed above our heads, and other times, it entirely envel-
oped our lives. Whenever my parents did reconcile and tried
moving forward, it took time for the tension to subside.

Despite the dysfunction in our home, I loved my parents
with the entirety of my innocent heart. I desperately desired my
parents' happiness and a sudden, miraculous capability to live
peaceful, content lives. The recurrence of such hurtful conflicts
reinforced the mantle's pressure of responsibility to perform my
task well and keep harmony within our home. I became disappointed in myself for not achieving the happiness I was destined
to bring to my parents. Even when I was told the opposite, I
continued to believe that their discord was all my fault.

My brothers, Micah and Zach, joined our family in 1999 and
2002, respectively. I will never forget the pride and excitement
I felt when I held each of my brothers for the first time, cra-
dling their delicate heads, smiling profusely at their little faces,

elated that I was granted the honor of being their big sister. But yet again, I grasped an undue mantle—this time to be the protective older sister.

For many years, I tried to shield my brothers from the hurtful effects of our parents' fighting. One day, when I was about nine years old, our parents' argument began to escalate. Micah, the headstrong toddler that he was, began to insert himself into the conflict. This made Mom and Dad even angrier, maneuvering around Micah as they rushed about the house, throwing insults at one another like a verbal boxing match. I knew I had to remove Micah from the situation, guard him from the emotional damage of our parents' controversy, and physically prevent him from engaging in their fight. I decided to take my brother upstairs to my bedroom where we could both find refuge from the chaos hastily moving downstairs.

It wasn't easy to convince Micah to leave the situation, and I brought him to my room throwing an absolute tantrum. When I closed my bedroom door and tried to explain to Micah, in the simplest of terms, why he needed to play in my room for the moment, he would not hear of it. My brother proceeded to push things off my desk and throw toys around my room until I let him free. As I reluctantly turned the doorknob and let my brother leave, he bounded out of my room like a deer fleeing oncoming headlights.

After Micah left, I sat on the floor in the middle of my room and cried. Not a silent, heartbroken cry, but one out of pure anguish and heartache, gasping for breath as each wail escaped my lips and my chest became so tight I believed I might just explode into thin air. My soul grieved for Micah. Why didn't he realize I needed to protect him? Micah didn't understand how emotionally damaging listening to our parents' fighting was, but I did.

One Sunday morning a few years later, we were getting ready to leave for church when my parents' fight escalated (again). Mom was sitting on the couch weeping, refusing to attend church. Dad seemed visibly angry with her behavior, haphazardly gesturing and pacing the living room, desperately imploring her to change her mind and come to church. But Mom refused his request. In a last attempt of persuasion, Dad grabbed Mom by the arm in hopes of removing her from the couch. He didn't grab her hard, nor were his actions successful, but the incident made Mom sob even louder. As Mom's tear-filled eyes met mine, her distress pierced my heart. In the past, I would've advocated for her reprieve, leaning into the mantle's support to resolve their conflict. But now, the mantle had destined another responsibility for me, one I was determined to uphold with absolute perfection: protecting my brothers. Immediately, I neglected Mom's plea for rescue, ignored Dad's frustration, picked Zach up into my arms, grabbed Micah's hand, and led my brothers outside into the peacefulness of the spring air.

I'm not sure how my parents' fight ended that day, if Mom came to church with us or if Dad took us on his own since the details sometimes blend in my memory. However, I can say I continued to protect my brothers as often as possible. Whenever I successfully shielded them from our parents' fighting, I felt satisfied. My life's objective adjusted to the responsibility of safeguarding my brothers' lives. Knowing that I was sacrificing myself to be there for Micah and Zach added to my life's value and purpose. If I thought the mantle was already a burden, I was certainly ambushed by the added strain of being responsible for my young brothers' innocence.

―――――――

There is one traumatic event in my life that ultimately changed the trajectory of my future, an incident of which I journaled:

"I guess I should write down the reason we came [to Pittsburgh] and how I felt. It might help someone later and might be a testimony..."

At the end of January 2006, my parents attended a prayer event about an hour from our home in Columbus. Being the responsible thirteen-year-old that I was, they trusted me to babysit my brothers (six and three years old at the time) while they were gone, assuring me of their return before the boys' bedtime. The few hours I watched my brothers that night were easy enough, although I was eager for my parents to come home so that I didn't have to watch *Walker Texas Ranger* anymore.

When Mom walked in the front door that night, exhaustion diluted every ounce of peacefulness from her presence. Immediately, Micah reminded her that someone (either Mom or Dad) told him they'd help build his new Playmobil castle before bed that night. Even though it was late, my mom conceded to the request, trying to keep the promise made to my brother. As Micah led Mom upstairs toward their building project, I asked why Dad hadn't come inside yet. Mom told me that he wanted to stay in a prayerful atmosphere and was going to drive around and pray a bit longer.

An hour later, Dad still wasn't home, so I decided to call him. I journaled our phone conversation:

"I asked, 'Where are you? What time will you be home?'
He said, 'I can't tell you. All I can say is I'm in a safe
place. I don't know when I'll be home.'
I said, 'Tell me where you are NOW! I'm scared!'
He still wouldn't."

I was absolutely terrified after this conversation. Hearing the dazed and placid sound of my dad's voice caused anxiety to rise within me—*where was Dad and why wouldn't he come home?* Two hours had passed since Mom began building with Micah, and the reality of bedtime was upon us. I journaled this part of the night's events:

"Micah <u>had</u> to go to bed, so Mom tried but he kept cry-
ing, saying 'I want my dad! When will he be home? I need
my daddy to say goodnight so I can go to sleep.' Mom was
<u>so</u> tired. Micah kept crying. I went [upstairs] to go to bed
and talk to Micah so Mom could get Zach to sleep."

After I talked with Micah and he settled down, I went to my room for the night, too. As I laid in bed, I sudden-ly heard Mom whispering loudly. I assumed Dad had finally come home, so I went to the edge of the stairs to listen. I heard Mom on the phone, scream-whispering, saying, "…it's 11:30, I'm tired, the kids aren't in bed…tell me where you are!" But Dad refused to tell her.

At 2:15 a.m., Mom woke me up because Dad *still* hadn't come home yet. She decided to go drive around and try to find him, so she wanted me to be awake in case my brothers woke up while she was gone. A half-hour later, she returned to no avail. We both returned to our rooms for solace and rest, but I'm not sure either of us found any.

In the morning, Mom told me that she had checked their bank account to see if Dad had gotten gas somewhere, what with all the driving and praying he was evidently accomplishing. Surprisingly, Dad did get gas at three different places during the night, and after mapping out their locations, my mom suspected that he had gone to North Carolina. The fact that my dad simply *left us* to go on an impromptu road trip and *refused* to tell us what he was doing was unexplainable.

In a desperate panic, Mom decided we needed to leave before Dad returned. Neither of us could predict what would happen when Dad came back, the instability of his behavior causing Mom to worry about our physical and emotional safety. I had my own concerns about Dad's return:

How would he act when he came home?

Was he safe to be around?

Why did he leave us?

Would my parents have a terrible fight when he came back?

Fear and confusion consumed me as I helped Mom pack our bags and escape to Gram's house. Gram lived several hours away in Pittsburgh, but it was the safest place for us to be amidst Dad's unpredictability.[1] My heart thumped with apprehension during the drive, the fear of how Dad would react

---

1. Gram is my mom's mom. She was a huge part of my life growing up, coming to visit us frequently over weekends and during holidays.

when he realized *we* had now left, the worry of why Dad was acting this way, and the nervousness of the unknown ahead consumed each thunderous beat.

Part of me was relieved we were escaping to Gram's because her house always made me feel comforted and secure. Growing up, I spent one week every summer in Pittsburgh with her, gallivanting across suburbia on entertaining adventures like visiting her classroom (an excursion that was work for her, but fun for me!),[2] going to feed the ducks at the nearby pond in North Park, picking up GG to get ice cream cones at Tastee-Freez, or spending a leisurely day in her backyard jumping on the trampoline.[3] Gram always found a way to have fun and make me feel special, like there was no one else in the world she would rather spend time with than me. That always made me feel really happy.

When we arrived in Pittsburgh, Gram welcomed us with open arms. Her living space was cramped, and beds were going to have to be shared, but the respite of her home was enough. My heart felt a little less terrified being at her house, knowing that peace and safety would surround us during this dismal moment in life. I was grateful for the reprieve.

The coming days after our escape were a blur. Dad was obviously upset when he returned home and realized we weren't there. He and Mom had several dramatic phone calls that tilted our family's world into a revolving panic. Despite the chaos, I cherished the stability we had at Gram's. A lot of what

---

2. Gram was an elementary music teacher for several years before transitioning to middle school chorus up until her retirement. Whenever I went along to school with her, I'd get to play with instruments or draw on the chalkboard while she accomplished whatever work she needed to do.

3. We'd often throw plastic miniature toys onto the trampoline, trying to bounce each one off without landing on them. Gram *always* jumped on top of multiple ones, grabbing her foot with a shout of *"Ouch! Ouch! Oh, Rebecca, this is not funny!"* as I laughed.

went on between my parents were "adult problems," things that I didn't need to know about or wouldn't understand because I was a teenager. However, the one circumstance I did find out about was the reason my dad left on that wretched night. Apparently, Dad was convinced of a spiritual conspiracy against him, and he thought it necessary to seek sanctum at a religious organization he knew of headquartered in North Carolina. When I learned the reason for our destined escape to Pittsburgh, I didn't know what to think. How does a thirteen-year-old girl wrap her head around the concept of irrational behavior, especially *spiritual* insanity?

A few months later, I journaled the details of that frightening night and my emotions toward my dad:

> *"I was so confused and hurt and angry. I was sad, too. I was **so** mad at Dad."*

My mom, brothers, and I spent five months living at Gram's, rebuilding a life without my dad—although he called us frequently and periodically visited. During our first few weeks in Pittsburgh, Mom had us join a local church, hoping to continue developing our personal relationships with Christ.[4] The church had a small congregation, mostly consisting of families who had been there since the early years of its beginning. It felt good to be in the comfort of a Christian community again. Although my time at this church wasn't perfect, my initial experiences alleviated a lot of the burdens I carried from

---

4. My parents had been a part of this congregation over a decade earlier and had maintained some ties to it throughout the years.

our transition to Pittsburgh. The opportunity to remove myself from the chaos and place myself in a positive environment uplifted my soul. Just like when I was a little girl, I found peace within the mortar walls of an ordinary building.

When I joined their youth group and entered the youth room for the first time—a large, open-concept space in the basement of the church furnished with mismatched couches, a ping-pong table, and blue folding chairs—I was surprised to be greeted by so many new peers eager to meet "the new girl."[5] Quickly, I made friends with most of the girls my age, developed a close relationship with the youth pastors, and began discovering more about my faith. In a matter of five months, I began attending services every Wednesday night, joined their worship team as a backup vocalist, volunteered at a Special Olympics event, went to a dodgeball fundraiser, and visited the beach—the most socialized experiences I had ever had! My involvement with the youth group's active community was a transformative opportunity during such an emotionally heavy time in my life.

Undoubtedly, the most important thing that came from my time in youth group was meeting my high school boyfriend, Jon.[6] Dating Jon was an unexpected decision, one that I was hesitant to accept yet desired with all my heart. Anticipating the beginning of our relationship made my teenage heart flutter, my stomach somersault with elation, and the excitement caused me to wonder—*why was I so happy about becoming Jon's girlfriend?*

I found out that Jon liked me during our youth group's trip to Ocean City, New Jersey. Well, if I'm honest, my mom

---

5. Little did I know that my future husband was the boy wearing the black hoodie reclining underneath the light switch in one of the blue chairs.
6. My high school sweetheart, best friend, soulmate, and *husband!*

thought he liked me a few months earlier, but I immediately dismissed her preposterous opinion because (as rumor had it) Jon already had a girlfriend from his high school.[7] I adamantly denied any feelings toward Jon, regardless of the butterflies I felt every time his name came up in conversation.

As fate would have it, the stars aligned on that beach trip, and our mutual feelings were made known.[8] During the five-and-a-half-hour car ride back to church, Jon typed a message on his phone, saying, *Can we talk when we get out of the van?* The excitement boiling inside my gut felt like it would bubble over, my heart gushing with anticipation for what Jon wanted to talk about. After we got to church and helped unload the van, I sat in the gazebo in the church's front yard, waiting for my mom to pick me up (and for Jon's inevitable question). Eventually, Jon found me waiting, and as he stepped into the gazebo, he struggled to maintain eye contact with me. Through his teenage nervousness, Jon quietly said, "So...are...we...", and I quickly answered, "Yeah, we are." Immediately, relief rushed across Jon's entire body as he lifted his head and smiled at me. I couldn't believe it—I had a *boyfriend*!

As young fourteen-year-olds, "dating" consisted of simply hanging out (constantly) together, getting to know each other, and becoming the best of friends. Our relationship was unlike anything I had ever dreamed of. Jon's expression of love, assurance, support, and adoration was so genuine that my heart could've burst from the positive enormity of it all. The negative views I had developed about myself defined my

---

7. I later found out it really was just a rumor.
8. In all transparency, Jon's feelings were much stronger than mine. Although I was interested in dating him, I was resistant to his genuine care for me. Throughout our relationship, I've struggled to accept his love and devotion because of the lessons I learned growing up, believing that I wasn't good enough to deserve true love.

value as ugly, shameful, disgusting, undeserving, and worthless. Dating Jon turned all those insecurities on their heads. I never believed that I was worthy of being unconditionally loved nor deserved to be treated with devotion and respect. Yet, my teenage boyfriend saw my value. Becoming Jon's girlfriend completely changed my life for *good*.

The expression of Christ that Jon has modeled throughout our eighteen-year relationship is the reason for so much of my success, happiness, and healing. Without Jon's Christlike love and unconditional support, I wouldn't be who I am today. Jon's devotion to always see the best in me has been a constant encouragement as I've pursued my dreams, accomplished goals, and found the courage to seek healing for the tender wounds of shame and despair from my past.

During the five months of separation, my parents had several conversations about our family's future. Inevitably, it was decided that Dad would move to Pittsburgh, and we would all live together again—one big, happy, dysfunctional family. Even though some relatives voiced their concerns about our family living together without proper resolution or therapy, I tried to support my mom through this difficult decision. My parents believed this was the best choice for our family, and I had to trust that they were right.

In July, Dad drove the moving truck filled with all the belongings we had frantically left at home, parking it in front of our family's new condo, ready for us to unpack the same baggage we had tried to escape from. As the five of us acclimated back to (un)stable life together, I was hopeful that things would be different. The thing about dysfunction is that unless intentional efforts are made to correct unhealthy habits, nothing changes.

I can't remember how long it took before my parents began fighting again, but the tension soon settled into our home like an ugly heirloom on display. I was frustrated to be in the same situation all over again, confused that such an epic low hadn't changed my parents' behaviors. I also resented Dad for leaving us. His actions were the reason we had to escape to Pittsburgh. He was the reason our family separated for five months. He made the insane choice to leave his family. Now that we were back together, why wasn't he trying to be better? Our family could've used this opportunity as a second chance for happiness. Why was the cycle of trauma repeating itself?

Moving from the security of Gram's house to the instability of our family's condo felt like a backward jump. I had gained so much from being away from the strife between my parents. Being back in an environment of constant worry and fear was dreadful. The mantle hadn't bothered me much while we lived with Gram, giving me a much-needed break from the pressure of perfection. But now, I had to carry it again; my family's happiness and my brothers' innocence depended on it.

I am so grateful that what was emotionally damaging to my innermost being brought me toward the refreshing outpouring of healing and happiness I've presently experienced. When I began my current journey of soul recovery, I read through Scripture and unpacked hopeful verses of love, truth, and wisdom that reflect God's perspective of my heartache.

Psalm 56:8 (NLT) says, "You keep track of all my sorrows. You have collected all my tears in your bottle. You have recorded each one in your book." Realizing that the Lord cares enough about me to collect my tears and record my sorrows brings comfort to my soul. When I go through hard things and feel the pressure of pain, loss, and offense, those experiences matter to God. The Lord does not inhibit bad things from happening on earth (hello, sin-filled world), but I believe that doesn't mean He destines troubled times to bring utter disaster in our lives, nor does He discredit the oppression and devastation of our experiences. Although this scriptural promise isn't one of deliverance, I find it profound because it is a promise of God's care for us. When I go through hardships, I can find consolation not just in knowing that the Lord is with me, but in believing that my sorrows and traumas are carefully noticed by Him, too. I may never understand the detrimental experiences I had throughout my upbringing, but I will always believe in God's merciful goodness. Knowing that every cry, every scream for justice, every miserable doubt of happiness were collected and held by my Savior makes all the difference.

About five years ago, a coworker expressed her astonishment after learning I had experienced a hard childhood. I was slightly surprised by her response, and then I realized how I must have appeared to her—so well-rounded, healthy, confident, capable, happy, mature. In all actuality, everything I am is because of God's redemptive grace. In 2 Corinthians 5:17 (NKJV) it says, "Therefore, if anyone is in Christ, he is a new creation; old things have passed away; behold, all things have become new." This verse is often referenced at the onset of one's salvation journey, representing that the blood of Jesus' sacrifice has washed away the old sinful life of the past. I never quite knew how to apply this scripture to my life because I had accepted Christ at the innocent age of three years old, and I didn't really have a sinful past to atone for. It wasn't until I began processing the burdens from my childhood that I realized the significance of this verse in my life.

For me, it wasn't about the transformation of my life's habits and decisions; it was about correcting the patterns of negativity I had learned from my environment and the mantle's pressure of perfection. I believe that being a "new creation" in Christ means that I have the ability to be different, renew my thoughts, and believe good things about myself and my life. Instead of believing in my human inadequacy, worthlessness, or inabilities, I've learned to redefine my life's value according to the standard of Christ's love, mercy, and grace. Each day that I choose to improve my thought patterns, believe in my self-worth, and place my value in the hands of Christ, I am *renewed*.

Chapter Three

The Road to Resilience

"Although the world is full of suffering, it is also full of the overcoming of it."

HELEN KELLER

The pig sat in the mud. Such a simplistic sentence, yet one that holds significant meaning in my life; this was the first sentence I ever read independently. As a young learner, I was excited to have achieved such an accomplishment! I recall the pride in my mom's voice as she praised me for my reading success. We immediately called GG on our landline to share the news of my first academic milestone. Little did I realize this was just the beginning of my complicated educational journey.

When I reached school-age readiness at five years old, my parents decided not to enroll me in the local public school system for kindergarten. The very thought of putting their innocent little girl on a huge, yellow bus with potential bullies and sending her into an educational institution that wouldn't value our Christian faith was unacceptable. Instead, my parents believed that a wholesome, Christian education at home would be beneficial for their impressionable firstborn.

Over the next decade, my mom and I ventured into the academic world of homeschooling. Our guest bedroom transformed into an amateur classroom with a singular open-front desk and a pint-sized chair stationed near the window, a laminated calendar set attached to the wall by gobs of sticky-tack, and a large bookcase stocked with curriculum resources, student workbooks, math manipulatives, and early readers. Within the comfort of our home, my mom became the pilot of my education. I experienced all the typical courses suggested for my grade level, although I never really knew what grade I was in because my schooling routine never drastically changed. I learned alone in the same room with the same teacher (who happened to be my mom) every year.

Our homeschooling routine was exceptionally flexible. Time did not constrain my learning, and instruction was fluid—detached from strict due dates or scheduled classes. Throughout my early elementary years, I participated in a local homeschool group. Homeschool groups are co-ops consisting of other homeschooling families that offer weekly classes, field trips, and other extracurricular activities. Every spring, the co-op families would meet at Slate Run Living Historical Farm to learn about the 1800s-run farmhouse, and in the fall, we would go to the Circleville Pumpkin Show and ride carnival rides together. On certain weekdays, our co-op participated in the local YMCA's swim, gym, and art programs. These activities provided an essential outlet for me and my homeschooled peers to socialize while learning new skills and experiencing life outside of our isolated classrooms.

As a young student, I had an enthusiasm for learning. I loved hands-on lessons when I could see, feel, and create physical representations of my understanding. During math, I made every excuse possible to use the red, blue, yellow, and green counting bears to help me visualize concepts. Sorting them by size or color, grouping them by quantity, and removing or adding bears to learn the basics of subtraction and addition made math an interactive experience. Once in kindergarten, I collaged a large cut-out of the letter *R* (the first letter of my first name) with photographs from magazines. I can't remember if the photos were of things that started with *R* or if they were pictures of things that I liked (since the letter was meant to be a representation of me), but either way, I was enthralled with the cutting and gluing aspect of the assignment. The independence of selecting any picture I thought was significant enough for the collage, then cutting it out with safety scissors and pasting it crookedly along the letters' straight sides made me proud.

Being an active learner was fun for my curious mind! I felt competent, capable, and pleased with myself whenever I successfully completed assignments and correctly understood learning objectives. However, as I continued through upper elementary coursework, my enjoyment of learning changed. Concepts became more complex and difficult to understand, and lessons shifted from hands-on activities to less interactive instruction.

I'll never forget the defeat I felt during a particular math lesson. No matter how hard I tried, my nine-year-old brain could not understand the concept of multiplication. My mom repeatedly explained the procedure, demonstrating how to solve using only my pencil and brain, saying how it was simply a faster way of adding groups of multiples. I knew how to add, so I could learn to multiply without manipulatives, no problem! But no matter how many examples Mom showed me, I just could not comprehend the strategy.

While the lesson dragged on, Mom and I grew impatient with each other. In my frustration, I began to test my mom's boundaries, complaining about the assignment and refusing to attempt the ridiculous work that I clearly could not learn. In response, Mom began huffing deep sighs of irritation, her voice becoming ridged as she repeated herself for the umpteenth time. As the tension mounted between us, I assumed it stemmed from my inability to process multiplication. I was discouraged by my stupidity, upset that I couldn't make my brain understand the concept, and disappointed that my incompetence also frustrated my mom.

When Dad came home from work that evening, Mom shoved the math assignment into his hands, stating something like, "You have to finish this with her," and then trudged upstairs for a much-needed break. I think I may have cried in protest for Mom to reconsider. Even though I assumed my attitude had agitated her, I still craved her support and wanted to please her by successfully finishing the assignment. Unfortunately, I had to let Dad help me instead.

While my dad helped me finish the lesson, I was surprised by his patience. It seemed like Dad understood my frustration and saw how difficult it was for me to comprehend. I could tell he was trying to support me as he took the time to read through the directions and sit with me as I processed each equation. Despite my dad's best efforts, I continued to struggle with the assignment. As time dragged on and bedtime soon approached, Dad's patience grew thin, and I gave up on ever understanding multiplication.[1]

Learning such daunting lessons appeared ceaseless along my grade-school journey. Comprehending abstract concepts, relying on rote memorization, and solving multi-step questions felt impossible. The more challenging subjects became, the more demoralized I felt. Once an eager, delightful, and curious learner at the beginning of kindergarten, I transformed into a discouraged, frustrated, and difficult student by the time sixth grade rolled around. I developed an intolerable attitude toward my schoolwork, which burdened my mom and prevented productive teaching. When I began middle-school curriculum, the pressure to educate me whilst raising my two younger brothers—a rambunctious preschooler and a happy-go-lucky toddler—was exhausting for my mom. Eventually,

---

1. I eventually did learn how to multiply, but it took many years and much practice before I mastered the concept.

Mom gave in to the pressure, and any progress toward a comprehensive education vanished from sight.

As a young pre-teen, I didn't understand the struggles my parents were facing in life, especially my mom. Around the time my regular schooling schedule ended, I sensed an air of sadness in the atmosphere of our home. My mom was always tired, unable to stay awake once the afternoon arrived, so I decided to step in and alleviate some of her burdens by supervising and caring for my younger siblings. Although I did make time for my own hobbies, I spent most afternoons with Micah and Zach, watching episodes of *Blue's Clues* and *Bob the Builder* on repeat and playing dinosaurs or building tracks for Thomas the Train cars. Dancing and singing along to the popular *Lights, Camera, Action, Wiggles!* movie was a highlight of our quality time together.

I gravitated toward the responsibility of taking care of my brothers. My role as the eldest sibling was a privilege, and the mantle took advantage of the pride I felt in being an older sister. Knowing that I was not only supporting my brothers but also helping my mom cope with whatever was bothering her boosted my self-esteem, too. Sometimes, being with my siblings felt tedious, but caring for my brothers brought much more fulfillment than annoyance to my life. I adored my siblings and was dedicated to doing whatever I could to love, protect, and care for them. Although I didn't always see it this way, my new responsibilities gave me a reasonable excuse not to focus on my middle-school studies. It was a relief to step away from the stress of academics. At the moment, I was pleased by the hiatus of a stable schooling routine, but my lack of education soon caught up with me.

Between sixth and ninth grade, my course load became so minuscule that I barely completed any academic lessons each month. When it was time to organize my yearly portfolio at the end of ninth grade, I embellished upon worksheets and assignments I had not really completed, fabricated some of the books on my reading log that I never actually read, and falsified the comprehensive education I most certainly did not receive. The lack of academic foundation and the minimal knowledge I acquired during those middle school years proved to become an immense hurdle in my self-confidence and later educational success.

Consequently, I developed a grotesque habit of skepticism and distress toward all things school-related. I was timid and ashamed anytime someone asked about my education or whenever academic concepts arose in conversation. Even though I was thrilled not to have an extensive course load compared to public school students, I realized the hindrance that such a knowledge gap created for me. Knowing I was missing vital components of my educational foundation made me feel stupid and embarrassed.

Before beginning tenth grade in 2007, my parents gave me the option to attend public school or enroll in cyber school. After our first year living in Pittsburgh, my parents decided that homeschooling wasn't the right fit for our family, thus presenting me with this momentous decision. At fifteen years old, entering a new social *and* academic situation felt too foreign from my comfort zone, so I chose to complete high school through enrollment in cyber school.[2]

Being a real student within a structured education system was an unbelievable experience. It was challenging acclimating to group instruction, adapting to structured class times, completing graded assignments, and receiving a grade point average. Balancing the routines and expectations of these new

---

2. I thought it was the least terrifying option, especially since it didn't require as much socialization or as frequent opportunities for my peers to realize how stupid I was.

school procedures put tremendous pressure on me to perform well and gain the approval of my teachers as a competent and hardworking student.

While building upon new knowledge, I was filling in the gaps in my academic foundation, trying to make up for those middle school years of sporadic learning. I frequently became frustrated with myself when I didn't understand a lesson or struggled to complete an assignment, and my lack of self-confidence reminded me of my stupidity and incompetence. The mantle latched onto these insecurities of imperfection, forcing me to compensate for not being smart enough. It pressured me to work diligently toward a comprehensive high school education despite my fragmented foundation.

At the end of my first year of cyber school, I wrote this journal entry:

"This 10th grade year was my first year of cyber school. It's been a few years since I've had real schooling. There were a lot of changes that I had to go through. When the school year first started, I would have panic attacks every night and every morning. But God helped me. He has helped me every single day of this '07-'08 school year. I have come out with high Bs and As."

That transitional school year was unlike anything I had experienced before. Every day, I prayed fervently to the Lord for peace, guidance, and support to conquer the demands of dread, worry, and panic. The pressure was so paralyzing at times that it hijacked every breath in my lungs, the angst racing in my heart so fast I thought it would beat right out of my chest. In those moments, I closed my eyes, attempting to release the tension, finding the ability to exhale with each methodical inhale. Amidst my nervous breakdowns, I chose to rely on the promise of Philippians 4:13 (NKJV) to get me through each day: "I can do all things through Christ who strengthens me."

Somehow, I found the strength to persevere through my first year of cyber school. I implemented regular routines, learned how to cope with due dates and graded assignments, and acclimated myself to the predictability and stability of disciplined schooling habits. Each day, I followed my course schedule, logged into my classes, made sure the internet was connected and the Wi-Fi was working, and adjusted the volume for my headset and mic.[3] Thankfully, the constant stress and staggering worry slowly diminished, and I found security in this new school environment.

Throughout high school, I mastered classes like American History, English, and Spanish II. With Jon's support, I also passed complicated courses like Chemistry, Algebra II, and Geometry. The structure and responsibility of cyber school instilled a self-motivational work ethic within me, and unexpectedly influenced the development of my self-identity and inner confidence. By God's grace, my intelligence transformed into something unrecognizable as I applied myself and began learning again.

⌖—⸱ ⸱—⌖

The transitional phase of adolescence—growing up and becoming a subordinate version of an adult—is commonly a dramatic, confusing, and awkward stage of life for every teenager. My experience was the same. My body was physically changing, morphing into this shapely, acne-prone, feminine

---

3. This was before webcams and Zoom calls.

figure, while my emotional being was refining itself, assessing the truth of my previously learned beliefs.

When I was sixteen years old, I began doubting the validity of my faith and the existence of God entirely. I don't remember the initial reason for my skepticism—perhaps it was just a natural response due to the emotional changes happening within myself. Whatever it was, something inside me decided that if I was going to become my own person, I needed reassurance in my own values and personal beliefs. This decision began with the testing of my faith.

As a child, I always felt safe, loved, and secure in my relationship with Christ, but as I began to examine my beliefs and discover my own identity, the simplicity of my faith seemed pointless. I determined that if God really was all that I had been taught to believe—loving, compassionate, forgiving, faithful, gracious, and righteous—then I wanted to discover His genuine character on my own terms. My goal wasn't to develop my Christian beliefs but to test and see if God was *real*. I determined that I didn't want to put forth effort in finding Jesus; I wanted Him to find *me*.

When I chose to pause my relationship with Jesus, I wasn't walking away from Christianity altogether. I still valued biblical morals and wanted to believe that *something* in the Bible was true. Throughout my childhood, being a Christian meant so much to me, like being awarded a gold star sticker for an achievement. Even though I didn't entirely dismiss my faith, I did adamantly reject a personal relationship with Christ. I stopped reading my Bible, listening to Christian music, and any other religious influence that had once uplifted my spirit.[4]

---

4. My parents expected me to attend church, so I went regularly, mostly to see my friends and spend time with Jon.

I may not have gone off the rails and become the world's worst sinner, but I definitely didn't want anything to do with Jesus— not until He proved Himself and found me in my hopelessness.

Coincidentally, an emotional heaviness consumed my spirit. It was like a protruding storm cloud overshadowed my life, full of depression and misery. The despair felt lodged within my heart, like a blockage so dismal it physically took over my emotional stamina.

During this time, my eleventh-grade English teacher was obsessed with the emo fad in the early 2000s and often discussed this interest during class. To be emo, one was typically labeled as *emotional,* owned a closet full of exclusively black clothing, and jammed out to hardcore punk rock. The quintessential persona of an emo person was supposed to be quiet, reserved, and shy. A classmate in my English class created an emo club, and every student who was emo placed a sad emoji beside their name icon to indicate their allegiance to the alliance. Outside of class, I had taken an "Are You Emo?" quiz on Facebook, and it stated I was "totally emo," validating my inclusion with my English class peers. [5]

I journaled this entry about my experience:

"...I got so excited because I would fit in with my English class! But, I kept saying over myself, 'I am emo. I am emo. I am emo,' and then it happened. I was already going through a hard time, that prophesying that over myself threw me into deep depression about life. I meant no harm in my words, but I did not understand their meaning."

---

5. Back in the day when you collected Flair buttons for your virtual corkboard and took quizzes for the thrill of it.

Although my fashion sense stayed the same and my music choice minimally wavered, I latched onto the spirit of being emo. I felt its dark, empty disposition seep into my skeptical heart, pouring its ignorance into my impressionable soul. Believing that I was emo intensified the depression I was experiencing from the seclusion of my faith, creating even more despair within myself.

Eventually, I could not bear the burden of such bleak hopelessness any longer, and I sought restoration in my relationship with Christ. The liberation of being in the Lord's presence had been missing from my life long enough, and I craved the security from living out my faith. I abandoned my skeptical attitude and clung to the irrevocable promises of God's redemptive grace, never-ending mercy, and abounding love. I discovered that the solution to my every longing for love, acceptance, and purpose was *Jesus*. Even though I had purposefully neglected Him and doubted His existence, God didn't just come to find me in my hopelessness, *He never left me*. And that's the most reassuring fact of all.

Throughout my life, I've exhibited many telltale signs of an abused child—chronic stress, anxiety, fearfulness, coping through imaginative scenarios, codependency, and low self-esteem. These signs developed from the dysfunctional environment of my upbringing and stealthily became enemies of my self-worth. As I journeyed between childhood and adolescence, my attitude soon turned negative, critical, and reserved. I'd express joy and love outwardly, but I had become dazed by doubt, confusion, and criticism.

Amidst this time of inner conflict about my self-worth, I met the biggest motivator to help me find my life's true value—Jon. A few months after we started dating, Jon and I were on the phone talking about nothing and everything as teenagers do. Offhandedly, Jon mentioned that he thought I was pretty. I wholeheartedly couldn't believe the sincerity of his words! I genuinely believed that I was quite the opposite of *pretty*. When I attempted to discredit his preposterous belief, I heard shuffling noises coming from the other end of my cell phone. When the rustling subsided, Jon began to read from a thesaurus every synonym for the word "*beautiful*"—Every. Single. One.[6] Jon said that unless I agreed with him, he would continue repeating each synonym until I believed I was pretty.

To this day, I am astonished by Jon's genuine admiration of who I am and how he has always valued every facet of me—my appearance, my intelligence, my personality. Beyond any shadow of a doubt, I would not be the woman I am today without Jon's love and support. I professed to him in my wedding vows, and I'll forever mean these words with all my heart: *Jon is God's greatest gift to me.*

Another person who positively influenced my self-confidence journey is my Aunt Emily.[7] Emily and I are only twelve years apart in age, and our relationship has always felt sisterlike with all the love and devotion a true sisterly bond can have. During her Matron of Honor speech at my wedding, Emily reminisced about the day I was born, saying, "I just knew that this little baby and I were gonna be great friends forever."

I've always admired my aunt's confidence and fun-loving nature. Her positive presence mesmerized me, especially as a

---

6. Yes, he read from a physical, paperback copy of an actual thesaurus. Can you believe the lack of technology in those days?!
7. Emily is my mom's younger sister.

little girl. Growing up, Emily always welcomed me into her teenage adventures, never minding if I was around and even letting me hang out with her and her high school friends. Despite all my insecurities, my Aunt Emily has always made me feel loved and accepted. To this day, the bond we share is a consistent source of support in my life.

An occasion that helped me begin to dismantle my perfectionist standards and find my self-confidence happened randomly in a Target parking lot with Aunt Emily.

I was about fifteen years old, and Emily had invited me to run errands with her. I was excited to spend time with her, gallivanting across suburbia to accomplish everything on her list. During our outing, it was past lunchtime, and our stomachs were both rumbling. Aunt Emily asked where I'd like to eat, so I offered my usual answer: "I don't know."[8] However, Emily is a strong-willed woman and a response of timidity wasn't going to be accepted.[9] She decided that if I wasn't going to offer a suggestion right then, I should wait in the car to think about it.

As Aunt Emily parked her gray Nissan Xterra and walked into Target, I sat in the passenger seat, fretting with anxiety. I couldn't handle the pressure of choosing a place to eat! What if I picked somewhere Emily didn't like? I was so used to complying with other peoples' preferences that suggesting my own felt uncomfortable. Emily expected me to have a decision by the time she finished shopping. What was I going to do?

When I saw Emily exit the store and start strolling back toward the Xterra, my nerves quivered with worry. I took a deep breath and rapidly exhaled my decision as she opened the car

---

8. The mantle's expectation for perfection frightened me to share my desires or think for myself, a residual effect of its pressure to please others.
9. If you ask my husband, strong-willed women run in my family.

door, blurting out, "I want a Happy Meal!" Instantaneously, Aunt Emily laughed while I waited nervously for her response.

With a loving smile, she said, "Okay, The Becca,[10] let's go get a Happy Meal!"

While my Aunt Emily drove us to McDonald's that day, I don't think the smile ever left my face. Her positive response showed me that my opinions are valuable, allowing my nerves to acclimate back to a peaceful rhythm. I realized that everything was turning out okay. Until that moment, I never realized that my ideas could be accepted without offending or upsetting someone else. Even though this was an insignificant decision—a minor opinion in the grand scheme of things—I was astonished by my bravery to express my own desire without someone else's prior approval. My choice to "go get a Happy Meal" helped me begin a journey of self-confidence to become my own person and find the value of my self-worth.

—♦— —♦—

At the end of eleventh grade in 2009, I was in anxious anticipation for the prospective changes with graduation and adulthood on the horizon. I journaled my woes in these two entries, saying:

> *"This has been a hard time for me; becoming an adult and knowing that my childhood is ending… The future is so unknown to me… This stage of life for me is full of deep faith in God…"*

---

10. Emily's adoring nickname for me. She says that because of all the challenges I've overcome in my life, I am a force of nature, hence *The* Becca.

"...I can tell you that the teenage years are very hard! So many new things are going on...just about everything in life it seems is out to get you, and life just seems so much harder than it used to be. Anyone can look in this [journal] at past entries and see how worried, stressed, confused, and depressed I've been. But, you can also look and see that the only thing that helps me through anything is God."

As my senior year of high school approached, the age-old question, "What do you want to be when you grow up?" pestered my thoughts. I had no idea what I wanted to be because I had never considered it. I didn't develop future goals or aspirations, and I never envisioned myself as anything except being "me" and raising a family.[11] The idea of becoming someone through a vocation and having a purpose outside of childrearing was mindboggling. I was also just beginning to distinguish between my true self-worth and the mantle's unrealistic expectations of perfection. I was finally discovering myself, yet the pressure to solidify my future plans weighed heavily on me. How was I supposed to figure out all these nuances in a year? Thankfully, I knew right where to turn for consolation and clarity: *Jesus.*

While figuring out my life's course, I relied on the truth found in Proverbs 2:3 (NLT), which says, "Cry out for insight and ask for understanding." I expended myself to find direction for my future in God's Word and prayed for guidance in God's plan for my life. I needed the Lord's insight to understand what I was supposed to do, who I was supposed to become, and how it was all supposed to happen. I knew

---

11. A role that I assumed every woman acquired based on my observations of families in my confined community.

that seeking the Lord was the best solution for my worries because He was the One who planned my entire life before I was even born! God created my purpose and existence, so why wouldn't I seek His counsel to solve this mysterious journey into adulthood?

I desperately desired for the words of Psalm 37:4 to come true in my future: "Take delight in the LORD, and he will give you the desires of your heart." My heart's desire was to accomplish God's will, continue finding my worth in His grace, and build my confidence through His love. But how to go about doing that remained a mystery. I constantly prayed for the Lord's direction and craved tangible answers, desperate for a flash of lightning to reveal the Lord's entire master plan for my life.

However, I learned that delighting in the Lord means much more than receiving concrete, precise answers to my deepest desires. Instead, God chose to take me on a more intimate journey where I learned to abide in Him and believe His promises would be fulfilled in due time because trusting God was my only option. Only then, when I placed complete faith in His actions, did I discover the clarity I desperately desired. I discovered that when I truly set my heart to delight in the Lord's unconditional love and unwavering faithfulness, He will answer my prayers and grant my heart's desires in His timing and in His perfect way.

In the middle of my senior year in January 2010, I told the Lord, "I don't have a plan for my life, but it seems like everyone else does," and I felt His Spirit speak these words: *You cannot plan out your future for I planned it long before you were born.*

Although this wasn't the revelation I hoped for, I chose to take refuge in the fact that it wasn't up to anyone else what I was supposed to become. The Lord's opinion was all that mattered. I knew that if I simply followed God's will and obeyed His guidance toward my future, every worry, doubt, and fear would be irrelevant. The more I trusted Him and relied on my faith, the more I began believing in myself.

As I continued to wait for God to unfold the details of my unknown future, I began to consider realistic options for my life after high school. My passion for caring for children and supporting others was my top priority, and as I contemplated my career opportunities, I focused on the possibility of either being a missionary or working in childcare.

During my early homeschooling years, an emphasis on missions was incorporated into my education. Mom and I would read various books about missionaries across the globe and throughout different decades, all sharing the gospel truth of God's love and displaying Christ's compassion through their selfless actions of care and acceptance to the communities they served. Our church's support of two local missionaries in Tibet reinforced my admiration for missionary work. I always loved the Sundays when the missionaries visited our church during their breaks from the mission field. They would dress in traditional Tibetan clothing and share special stories about the local people and the advancement of the gospel in the Tibetan community. My family always received an updated prayer calendar and brochure about their local mission work, and we would prioritize prayer for their ministry and the country of Tibet during my school routines.

The children's ministry at our church also incorporated awareness of missionary work. I'll never forget when a fellow church member was invited to speak during our children's church service. She had recently returned from a missionary venture in China, but instead of simply sharing her testimony and presenting a speech about her life-changing adventure, the church member designed a course around our church's property and took the elementary kids on a simulated experience of the underground church. I remember feeling nervous as we crept from one hiding place to another, quietly tiptoeing through the hallways, stealthily sneaking in and out of exits whenever the coast was clear, the adrenaline racing in my heart as volunteers impersonated government officials and arrested us for holding a secret church service. I was astonished by the cruelty against believing something so pure as the gospel.

During high school, I had the privilege of attending several mission trips organized by a different church we attended.[12] Each trip provided amazing experiences to see other cultures, contribute toward community outreaches, and share the gospel's transformative message of love and redemption. Leaving my comfort zone and traveling to serve those less fortunate than myself was the most humbling and inspiring thing I had ever done.

Worship services at the local churches were incredible, much different from those I frequented in the States. The music quality was typically subpar, the chairs were plastic and mismatched, the room was cramped, and sweat from the humidity often stained your favorite t-shirt. But none of that mattered as our communal praise filled the room with rejoicing! The unity between people of different cultures coming together to worship God so freely was beautiful.

The connections made with people during these trips were a highlight of the experience. Much of our time was spent evangelizing to locals, leading church services, assisting

---

12. I traveled to Mexico once and Guatemala twice.

children's activities, or helping churches with construction projects. However, during one mission trip to Guatemala, our team visited a local orphanage. It was not a typical stop for a ministry venture, but the opportunity was offered, and our team eagerly accepted. We didn't spend much time at the orphanage, but the quality time we did have was unforgettable. Some of the children were hesitant to interact with us strange Americans, while others were intrigued by our accent, language, and appearance. Despite the language barrier, many of the children joined in a game of hacky sack with the teenage boys on our team, while others simply shared laughs and smiles with the rest of us, creating an unspoken bond between us all. Although our time at the orphanage was short, our connection with the orphans was profound. Many of our team members left the visit with tear-filled eyes and heavy hearts from the emotional impact. Being a part of a missions team and working together to serve others in need brought me closer to the Lord and influenced my desire to care for others.

As a teenager, I had an innate desire to help others and care for children. I gained a lot of experience working with young ones through babysitting, helping in the nursery at church, assisting at a monthly mom's group, and constantly overseeing my brothers. My favorite thing about caring for young children was the responsibility of supervising their play and the constant movement of their routines. Anytime I soothed a sobbing baby, changed a dirty diaper, heard a tickled belly laugh, or read aloud a book during nap time, I felt privileged to be a part of something so important as their developing lives.

During my senior year of high school, I had a regular babysitting job for a homeschooling family. Several mornings each week, I went to their home to supervise their young, adventurous toddler while his mom devoted uninterrupted time to teaching his two older siblings. One day, we played trains together, pushing the locomotives back and forth along the carpeted tracks of the living room, exclaiming, *"Choo, choo!"* in unison as our trains rushed past each other. As we played, I decided to mention the color of my railcar, saying something like, "Here comes the blue train!" Soon enough, my young protégé decided he wanted to switch railcars, and when he grabbed the blue train from my hand, he held it high up in the air and shouted, "Blue!" I was so proud of him for recalling the color I had mentioned while we casually played together. When I reached for the train he had been using, I told him it was the color "green," to which he enthusiastically repeated "Geen!" in his adorable two-year-old voice.

That moment showed me the simplicity of an educational foundation and the importance of learning through play. Facilitating lessons through daily activities helped me realize the value of basic yet comprehensive milestones for young children. Observing the pride in a young child's eyes when they learn something new and watching those "lightbulb" moments of awe and delight ignite throughout their expressions were gratifying experiences. Being with young children made me feel fulfilled.

I wasn't sure where the Lord's plan would lead me after high school, but I believed it could include my passion for missionary work or childcare. Either way, I knew God had destined something special for my future, I just didn't know what it was yet, and the anticipation consumed me.

I graduated from high school on a rainy day in June 2010. This was a day I never dreamed of achieving while being homeschooled—the idea that I would wear an official cap and gown and get to walk across an auditorium stage to receive a diploma.[13] Although cyber school was entirely virtual, an in-person ceremony was hosted at the downtown Soldiers and Sailors Memorial, an elegant venue for an unimaginable milestone in my life. Through all the bumps and hurdles of my academic journey, I was proud to graduate with average grades and a profound work ethic of independence and self-motivation. I wasn't sure what would happen after I flipped my tassel and walked off stage with my hard-earned diploma, but I knew the confidence, lessons, and experiences I gained from those three influential years of cyber school had changed the trajectory of my future success.

As time ticked past and senior year ended, decisions for my future were impatiently knocking at my door. Five days after my high school graduation, I began to verbalize my heart's deepest desire as I journaled:

> "Right now my passion is not missions, but children...here in the USA...I feel like I need to view my country as a mission field, not just go on mission trips."

After confessing my aspirations to the Lord, abounding excitement consumed my soul. This was the direction I intensely sought after; I wanted to make a difference by serving my local community and working with children.

A few weeks later, I told my parents that I was not going to become a missionary and wanted to work with children locally

---

13. Homeschool co-ops typically have intimate, unofficial graduation ceremonies.

instead. To say my mom and dad were disappointed with my decision is an understatement; they were furious.

During one of my mission trips to Guatemala, I learned about an opportunity to intern with the local missionaries there. My parents had urged me to apply, believing that being a missionary was God's call on my life. This new aspiration of mine to stay in the States did not align with their vision for my future. Mom and Dad were concerned about the reality of my decision because I didn't have an exact plan about what working with kids would look like. All I knew for sure was that God wanted me to serve children here at home.

My parents' opposition toward my future caused great tension between the three of us. I wrote this journal entry soon after our disagreement:

> "Things with my family and my future are really not going well, and as I was praying, I felt like the Lord told me to read 1 Thessalonians 5:19, which says 'Do not hold back the work of the Holy Spirit.'"

I truly felt that I was obeying the wisdom of the Holy Spirit guiding me to work with children. He may not have given me a physical map showing how to achieve my life's purpose, but I knew that God would continue to lead me as I figured it out. This was what I was meant to do with my life, and I didn't understand how my parents could act so defiantly toward God's will.

◆——— ———◆

Growing up, the relationships I developed with my parents were complete opposites. Although my dad tried to initiate a relationship with me when I was a little girl, an attachment never grew between us. On the contrary, I developed a faithful connection to my mom from an early age, a bond of love, security, and dependability. During my childhood, I lived to bring my mom happiness, trying to compensate for my existence, desperate to connect with her and prevent any unhappiness from shattering her life further. It was like an invisible umbilical cord connected my subconscious to Mom's emotions, causing me great distress when she was sad and immense pleasure when she was happy.

When I was about eight years old, Mom briefly worked a night shift at Walmart. One night, I was upset that Dad had to put me to bed while Mom was at work. In protest, I stayed up a bit later, tears streaming down my face as I sat on the edge of my bed and looked out the window, peering into the gray, hazy evening, wishing Mom was there. At that moment, I grabbed a journal from my nightstand drawer and began writing a song of intense sorrow, describing my woes of missing Mom and being unable to say "good night" to her. Silently, I wept, crocodile tears lunging onto the pages of my handwriting. Although I no longer have the original copy, I remember the song had multiple verses of emotional supplication, such as, *"I wish, I wish, I wish my mom was here to say good night,"* each lyrical line sung in a young, woeful falsetto.

As I entered adolescence, I became a confidant for Mom, someone she could rely on to support her by helping around the house, cooking dinner, or caring for my younger brothers. Whenever I could relieve my mom of any pressure or stress, I felt invincible. I often described Mom as *my best friend* for her constant companionship, a relationship that I genuinely treasured. Whenever we spent time together doing things we mutually loved, like our seasonal shopping excursions, playing Gin Rummy after my brothers went to bed, or choreographing a new human video skit for the church's drama team, I felt happy and fulfilled. It was as if my valiant efforts were finally paying for the misfortune of my existence, bringing pleasure and happiness to both Mom and me.

Amidst the conflict of my post-graduation decision, I desperately wanted my parents to understand why I felt the Lord calling me to work with children. I decided to talk with my mom privately about my decision. Because of the present tension between us, I was nervous to share such an intimate revelation with her. However, I wanted to open the door of communication and tell her more about what I believed was God's plan for my life, especially since my mom was *my friend*.

As I shared, my energy surged with enthusiasm and hope. I was eager to exclaim it from the rooftops, the reality that I was about to begin God's predestined plan for my life! However, the sharp sway of my mom's head and the stern expression of disparity glazed across her face quashed my optimism. In response, my mom told me, "God has better for you," and dismissed my hope. I felt confused, heartbroken, and grieved by Mom's disapproval. Why did she refuse to listen to me? Didn't she believe me?

After this discouraging conversation, I determined that my parents were not willing to support the future I wanted to pursue, and I decided to limit what I shared with them about my plans. Instead, I sought support from other people in my life who offered encouragement and affirmation, leaving the frustration and confusion of the situation to simmer between my parents.

At the beginning of my senior year, I had mentioned to my parents the possibility of moving in with Gram after I turned eighteen and graduated. Gram lived only twenty minutes away from my parents' house, and during high school, I often spent weekend nights at her place since it was near Jon's home. Surprisingly, my dad said he was open to the conversation; however, my mom had given him the most lurid glare, her eyes wide, lips tight, chin rigid. That was the end of our conversation…until I graduated.

Moving into Gram's house seemed to be the perfect solution. I would have a safe space to begin the next phase of life away from the dysfunction of home. Since I was officially an adult, I believed I had the right to decide what to do with my life, especially since I was prioritizing the Lord's wisdom for guidance about my future. I tried my best to communicate with my parents because I didn't want to disrespect them, but they were too hurt and upset to reciprocate kindly.

To my parents' dismay, I found support in my close relationships with Jon, Aunt Emily, and Gram. Whenever I shared my feelings with them, their reactions resounded in encouragement. The constant positivity and belief in my resiliency made me feel valued and capable. From my parents' perspective, I was plotting my future behind their backs, therefore acting disobedient by discussing my intentions with everyone close to me except for them. When I began excluding them from my plans, they felt disregarded and slighted, but I felt like all they expressed was opposition and displeasure toward my obedience to God's will. I came to a crossroads where I had to choose whether to follow the guidance of the Holy Spirit and what I believed I was supposed to do with my life or obey my parents' beliefs regarding my future path. Although my intentions were sincere, I know that disconnecting from my parents was hurtful and confusing to them.

⋖⊷— ⊷⋗

Two years later, I wrote this journal entry in reflection on this time of conflict between my parents and me:

"[Dad] would call me and yell at me for being disobedient and making wrong decisions and not seeing the truth. He would just keep talking and yelling without any response from me as I cried silently. Once I got off the phone with him each time, I'd go into a fit of tears. It physically hurt me to go through this with my parents. I had such peace about my decision and all the yelling, negative comments, disappointments, and withdrawal my parents expressed toward me made my heart physically hurt. God gave me such strength to go through that time. Sometimes I forget how hard and life-changing it was…"

That post-graduation summer of 2010 was emotionally eventful, to say the least. Jon had been going through health issues involving terrible stomach pain and bleeding. Doctors recommended procedure after procedure, test after test, possibility after possibility until it was decided that Jon would have surgery to remove polyps in his stomach.[14]

His surgery was scheduled for July, right at the height of this conflict between my parents and me. The timing felt like complete chaos. All I wanted was to support my boyfriend

---

14. Which the doctors discovered during surgery weren't *really* there, but at least they successfully completed an appendectomy instead of curing Jon's prolonged pain and bleeding. I digress.

and see him through a healthy recovery. Meanwhile, it seemed like my parents were obtruding their disappointment and frustration with my future plans at every possible moment. I'll never forget getting a call from my dad while I was visiting Jon in the hospital. The anxiety I felt each time I saw Dad's name appear on my phone was suffocating. I ignored the call but later listened to the long, drawn-out voicemail that practically disowned me as his child, telling me to come pack up my things and move out already because my parents would not condone such disobedience and disrespect.

During another hospital visit that week, I answered a call from my mom wanting to discuss my future plans. As I tried to explain the importance of being present to support Jon at that moment, Mom yelled at me, shouting, "Bull crap, Becca! That's just bull crap!" It hurt my heart beyond words to receive such resentment from my parents; it felt like a repeated physical punch to the gut. I had such peace and confidence that the overt ridicule from my parents was debilitating.

On the day of Jon's stomach surgery, my parents scheduled a meeting for me to attend with them and their pastor to discuss my post-graduation decisions. I protested and begged them to talk to me without their pastor's input, but they insisted. In hopes of helping my parents understand my decision, I hesitantly agreed to the meeting.

Since our move to Pittsburgh, my family had been a part of this church for four years. The pastor had taught my youth group Sunday school class, and I always had desired to build a relationship with him because he was held in such high regard by numerous church members (including my parents) and many of my peers in youth group. Once in high school, on one of our "monthiversaries," Jon and I asked the pastor to pray for us because we wanted Christ to be the center of our relationship. The pastor appeared suspicious of our request—I assume he thought perhaps we had *sinned* and therefore required penance for our wrongdoing—and warily prayed over us. I didn't understand why the pastor appeared so disinterested in knowing Jon and me. I was confused by his apparent mistrust of our dating relationship and consequently learned to distrust him, too.

As I walked into this dubious meeting, I felt overly cautious (and sick to my stomach). During the meeting, the pastor explained that because he had close relationships with my parents, that meant he knew me, too. He proceeded to raise his voice and *yell* at me for the disobedience I was showing my parents in the choices that I was making. I was flabbergasted by his arrogance to assume that he had *any* right to speak into my life with no personal relationship with me *and* that he believed it was appropriate to *shout* his judgments at me. I was floored.

My parents proceeded to sit there, listening to the disparaging banter spewing from their pastor's lips, as I also sat there, my blood boiling hotter than ever. I could not believe what was happening! Not once during that meeting was I able to speak my truth and reveal the wisdom God had provided to guide me. Their pastor assumed he knew the entire truth of the situation because he had spoken with my parents, never once considering a talk with me about my perspective.

To this day, I've never been so disrespected and demeaned by someone outside of my family circle as I was during that meeting. I felt hurt, betrayed, and degraded by my parents and their pastor's actions that day. The repercussions of this meeting solidified what I already knew: I was entering adulthood without my parents' support.

After the meeting, I drove back to the hospital with tears streaming down my cheeks, my heart mournfully accepting the reality of my parents' disapproval. For eighteen years, I tried to atone for my parents' happiness, and now my decisions were breaking their hearts. Feelings of shame, disappointment, and regret consumed my soul for not being the redeeming daughter Mom and Dad needed, a role I had held in high esteem for as long as I could remember. Yet, deep in my heart, I knew I was doing the right thing for *me*. My life was now mine to shape and experience without anyone else's permission. I knew God was leading me into my unknown future, and I was doing the right thing by obeying the Lord's will for my life, even if my parents disagreed.

Several weeks later, I moved out of my parents' home and into Gram's. It was one of the hardest things I had ever done. I hated leaving on such negative terms with Mom and Dad, feeling like I was abandoning my brothers in the turbulent environment. The longer I sat in the pain, the more selfish I felt for leaving. I even doubted my decision, wondering if my actions really were disobedient toward my parents. Their strong disapproval of my plan to move out and not become a missionary weighed me down. As I debated the consequences of my choices, I reaffirmed that I wasn't being disobedient toward my parents; I was being obedient to God. I realized that pleasing my parents was no longer a burden I could carry. If I was going to successfully pursue the future God had for me, I needed to let go of the mantle's unrealistic expectations. Moving out was the first step to destroy its snide intentions of perfection.

To further eliminate the mantle's stronghold in my life, I had to correct my belief that I was destined to be the protector and caretaker for my brothers. Being a big sister meant everything to me. The responsibility to model good behavior, care for my brothers' needs, supervise their play, and safeguard their innocence from the aggression in our home was a huge role I took very seriously. Deciding to move out of my parents' house wasn't a decision I made lightly, especially considering the impact it had on Micah and Zach. If I wasn't home, who would protect them from our parents' fighting, help them learn and grow, or mediate their brotherly quarrels? As a big sister, I was supposed to love, care for, and support my siblings, but not to the level of intensity I had reached. The mantle twisted my good intentions into an ambition for perfection. Realizing that the fulfillment I felt by shielding and taking care of my brothers came from the mantle was a difficult truth to process.

If I was going to proceed with the Lord's plan for my life, I knew I had to release these feelings and accept that everything was in God's hands. As I tried to remove the mantle's sacred overlay of perfection and atonement, I no longer found my worth in its pleasing expectations but in the significant purpose of my future ahead.

I began devising a plan of action for my career endeavors. With my high school diploma, working with children meant becoming a full-time nanny or a daycare teaching assistant. If I wanted a more distinguished position, such as a classroom teacher or center director, I would need to consider getting a college degree. The idea of *me* attending college was preposterous! Being a college graduate with a hard-earned degree was not something I imagined my insecure, academically challenged self able to become—not in my wildest dreams! Yet, the desire to be a teacher steadily grew within me.

In preparation for whichever career direction I chose, I decided to find a job working in childcare. That fall, the Lord blessed me with two part-time jobs at reputable childcare facilities, and my passion for the field of education blossomed. I enjoyed my role as a teaching assistant, supporting learning in the preschool-age classrooms and helping care for the basic needs of each child in the toddler and infant rooms. Every bottle I gave, baby I cradled, hands I helped wash, song I sang, and craft I supervised brought me such joy. I admired watching the classroom teachers instruct their students and care for the little ones, and I appreciated all that I was learning from observing their unique classroom management styles and perfected teaching techniques. After three months as a teacher's assistant, I knew I wanted to pursue a college degree and become a teacher.

In January 2011, I enrolled at the local community college and became a part-time student. I journaled my gratitude to the Lord, saying:

> *"Thank you. Thank you for my two jobs. Thank you for making them work with my schedule. Thank you for helping me pull through the hard patches. Thank you for my schooling opportunity. Thank you for my classes. Thank you for my teachers. Thank you for working everything out. Thank you for being here."*

I couldn't believe all my success and the goals I was reaching! Over the next sixteen months at college, I was inducted into the honors society for my perfect grade point average and was awarded two scholarships through the education department. After my fragmented grade-school experience and the knowledge gaps I had struggled to fill during cyber school, seeing the Lord's faithfulness materialize was unbelievable. I felt humbled, grateful, and incredibly proud to be living such a blessed life! I had no doubt that my confidence was spurred by my faith in the Lord's plan for my future. He had spoken to my heart, guiding my desires toward these very opportunities, and I was thriving!

Despite these positive experiences, I continued to struggle with the mantle's lasting implications of perfectionism. I expected excellent efforts from myself to accomplish goals in every aspect of life. While I began working and started community college, I was determined to be accepted as a valuable, hard-working, and competent employee, colleague, and student—but my definitions of those titles were harsh and unrealistic. Whenever I faced a conflict or didn't receive a perfect score on an assignment, I believed I wasn't performing to the best of my capabilities (or rather, the expectations I assumed I should achieve), nor was I portraying the best version of *me* possible (or how I presumed others expected me to be). If I made a mistake, didn't understand something, or missed points on an exam, I felt like a complete failure. I was disappointed in myself for not doing better, discouraged by my lack of knowledge and expertise. The pressure to flawlessly perform was only aided by the haunting words from my dad during that previous summer: "You'll fail, Becca. You'll fail."

Weeks before I moved out, I came home from visiting Jon one night to (yet again) discuss my post-graduation plans with my parents. However, on this particular night, Dad informed me that Mom was so upset with me that "she [couldn't] even look at me," so I would have this conversation alone with him. As I sat poised on the couch, prepared to explain my plans and honest intentions about my future, Dad became entirely consumed with rage, frantically pacing the living room, blathering on and on regarding my disobedience, hysterically gesturing, anger fuming red across his exasperated face as he passionately whisper-yelled at me (as not to wake my sleeping brothers). All I could do at that moment was sit in complete shock as I watched my dad explode, listening to him ridicule my "rebellious" behavior.

As this astonishing scene continued, my dad briefly paused from his pacing. He deliberately stood in front of me, hunched over to establish eye contact, pointed his index finger in front of my face, and shook it as he said, "Okay, okay, you go ahead with your plans. You'll fail. You're going to fail." Immediately, Dad resumed his hectic pacing and furious whisper banter, cruelly exclaiming, "I'll raise my sons better than I raised you!" I was so stunned by my dad's contempt that I simply laughed; I didn't know what else to do! Did my dad really just wave his finger in my face and tell me I would *fail*?! It was unbelievable. And it hurt. Deeply.

Every time I attempted to succeed and was met with adversity, I'd remember my dad's words because that was my ultimate fear; I didn't want to *fail*. During my first semester at community college, I received a C on an assignment for not answering several questions completely. Even though this was an honest mistake made on a trivial ten-point assignment, I felt humiliated and discouraged. I wrote this journal entry afterward:

"Every time I do 'worse' than the best, I remember my dad's finger shaking in my face, saying in confidence, 'Okay, you'll fail. You will fail.' I have to prove him wrong."

Any ounce of confidence was shattered every time I remembered my dad's words. Oppressive doubt consumed my mind as I wondered if I really was resilient enough to overcome struggles and accomplish my dreams of being a teacher. Was I smart enough? Capable, competent, strong, wise, gifted enough to succeed in college and become a qualified educator?

In these moments of complete disparity and self-loathing, I wrestled with the sincere truth that God predestined a *good* future for me, confounded by the idea that He created me *exceptionally* special. Psalm 139:13-14 says, "For you created my inmost being; you knit me together in my mother's womb. I praise you because I am fearfully and wonderfully made; your works are wonderful, I know that full well." Processing the truth of this scripture helped me realize the significance of being hand-crafted by God.

Understanding that every piece of me—my mind, body, and soul—was designed and structured by the Creator of the universe was astonishing. Everything that God has made is created with intention, love, and excellence, and I struggled to accept that His wonderful works included *me,* too. I had grown up with such belittled self-confidence, constantly devaluing my worth and capabilities, that choosing to believe this biblical truth felt nearly impossible. It was bewildering to think that despite my failures, insecurities, lack of self-esteem, physical flaws, and self-degrading attitude, God made *me* wonderful. Every strand of hair, every skin cell, every emotion within myself, every breath in my lungs, every detail was woven together by God to create something *good*. How inspiring is that?! I discovered that when I feel discouraged, worthless, disappointed, or inadequate, there is power in reminding myself of who God created me to be—worthy, wonderful, chosen, and loved.

Ephesians 2:10 proclaims, "For we are God's handiwork, created in Christ Jesus to do good works, which God prepared in advance for us to do." The incredible truth is that God not only created us with intention, but He also specifically planned our lives for a purpose. I believed that God's plan for my life was to become a teacher. Every passion, talent, gift, and interest I had pointed toward a career in education. I wasn't sure how the details would fall into place, but I hoped that if this was the Lord's will for my life, He would make it happen.

In my humanness, I've struggled to accept the reality that God prepared good works for me to achieve, doubting my self-worth and ability to fulfill my life's calling. But, as I continuously choose to rely on the Lord's promises, reminding myself of the quality work He designed through my giftings and capabilities, I'm reassured of what God believes about me and the destiny I am meant to pursue. I believe that in every part of our lives, during the most blissful chapters, the greatest heartbreak, and most challenging seasons, we must cling to the promises of God's Word and remember who He has created us to be—*fearfully* and *wonderfully* made *masterpieces* created for a *good* purpose!

Chapter Four

The New Trajectory

"And in the end, maybe it's not what God is working on but how God is working in us that matters most of all."

LYSA TERKEURST

The dreaded soccer game weekend. The game itself wasn't bad. I found it amusing watching adorable eight-year-olds learn to maneuver the ball down the field, pass it to their teammates, and score a goal. What made it even more entertaining was watching my youngest brother, Zach, hustle and support his team. He's the reason I went to these soccer matches. Any weekend that his indoor league had a game, Gram and I would be there to cheer him on! But I dreaded seeing my parents there. It was hard to experience such disregard from them as they often ignored my presence. The anxiety of being with them, several inches from each other, breathing the same air, and feeling completely cold-shouldered was emotionally overwhelming.

After moving out, I tried to remain part of our family unit—attending Zach's soccer matches and Micah's basketball games, going to see my brothers' school concerts,[1] tagging along on weekend excursions, or participating in holiday traditions—but it felt awkward being with my parents. The atmosphere was saturated with hurt, confusion, and disapproval about my post-graduation choices. Regardless of how nervous I felt around my parents, I knew I needed to keep showing up for my brothers' sake.

Despite my current relationship status with my parents, I desperately wanted to still be a part of my brothers' lives. Micah was eleven and Zach was almost eight years old when I left home. I didn't know how to communicate my decision to them, how to explain the complexities of purpose, choice, God's plan, and family dysfunction. I had dedicated eleven years of my life to sheltering and looking after my brothers, and

---

1. When I started cyber school in 2007, Micah enrolled in second grade at the local public school, and Zach started preschool at our church.

it felt wrong to leave without their understanding. Sacrificing my job as protector and caretaker, a role I held with utmost esteem, was the hardest thing I had ever done.

I missed a lot while my brothers grew up. There are times Micah and Zach will reminisce about life, many of the day-to-day moments during their childhoods and high school years that I wasn't there for. Even though I tried to be a part of their lives, not being at home affected the closeness of our relationships. Part of the reason it was difficult to remain close was because of our age differences—when Zach was finishing middle school, I was beginning my marriage—but most of it was because I began to pursue my own life while my brothers became their own persons without me around. When I think about this, guilt creeps into my soul like a vicious prosecutor, accusing me of not being there to support my brothers. In the pit of regret, I have to remind myself that my purpose was never to be the protector of my siblings; I was meant to simply be their *sister*.

During this awkward time, I did my best to spend quality time with my brothers. Aside from prioritizing their sporting games and school events, I'd take them out for lunch at Sir Pizza or come to the house to play with their new dog, Thumper. Anytime I could be with Micah and Zach and show them that I cared was important to me. I knew that when I moved out, it seemed like I had completely vanished from their lives. From their perspectives, it was as if one day I was home, a part of the family, and the next day I was gone, only seeing them for scheduled visits. It still saddens me that this was the reality of not living at home while pursuing my dreams.

Now that we're all adults, I'm blessed to have personal relationships with Micah and Zach. We talk regularly, chit-chatting about the latest news in our lives, supporting each other through the trials of adulthood, sometimes discussing the past and the life lessons we've learned from those difficult years. Whenever I connect with my brothers, whether we're talking, laughing, complaining, or reminiscing, I am eternally grateful for the close bond we now share.

I know I haven't been a perfect older sister, even when I was striving toward the mantle's standard of perfection. But I've always tried to be there for my brothers, and I think that's what has made a difference in our relationships. Even when I was venturing off attending college, starting my career, and getting married, I let Micah and Zach know that I would always be there for them, someone who would listen, offer advice, give support, affirm their efforts, and love them. That's my purpose as a big sister. I may have fallen short as the protective older sibling I wanted to be, but now, I'm a friend they can rely on, and that means everything to me.

Amending my relationships with my parents was a complicated journey. The disunity between Mom, Dad, and me lingered for some time as I went along my career path and kept attending family functions. Eventually, it seemed like my parents were trying to sustain somewhat of a relationship with me (although still upset and disapproving of my choices). Despite the awkwardness, I wanted to feel like a family again. Even if it was dysfunctional, this was my family, and I loved them.

About six months after my big move, something happened between me and Mom. Later, I found out someone told her inaccurate details about my life, causing my mom to believe I was dishonest with her. She suddenly became very distant, refusing to make eye contact, limiting communication, and didn't even call me on my nineteenth birthday. I thought we were making strides in our relationship, and I was confused by the abruptness of her indifference. Even though we disagreed about my adulthood choices, I still wanted Mom to be a part of my life. I loved my mom deeply, and her unexplained absence was distressing.

That summer of 2011, Mom and I began emailing and sending letters to each other, explaining our own sides to the complex story of our current relationship. It was emotionally strenuous communicating this way, feelings of dread, hurt, confusion, and love entangled within my heart. I wanted to be honest with my mom and communicate openly. It meant so much to me when she wrote about how proud she was of me, how she'll always love me, and that she wanted the best for my future, even if we disagreed. Knowing Mom did care and was willing to take the uncomfortable steps necessary to improve our relationship was a welcomed relief. I appreciated the vulnerable position Mom put herself in to be transparent with me. I was proud that we both chose to talk through our feelings and discuss the difficult circumstances between us. Our relationship was important to me, and I was grateful for the opportunity to rebuild it.

As for Dad, it was hard for me to consider having a close relationship with him. The constant fighting between my parents, our epic escape to (and reunification in) Pittsburgh, and Dad's cruel comments after I graduated were huge factors that influenced my distrust toward him. Although he did apologize for the trauma of my childhood and the hurtful things he said to me, I knew it wasn't enough to solve the problems of our severed relationship. I wanted to believe that his apologies were true, that we could fix our relationship, and Dad could be the father I needed. I tried to talk to him about the past and how his actions made me feel, but those discussions never sustained the longevity of a healthy relationship. Dad would become fixated on his own beliefs or disregard the boundaries that I requested, making it impossible for me to feel safe and loved during our conversations. Dad began the habit of promising things wouldn't happen again, then apologizing after they did. Eventually, the cycle of letdowns became too much for me, and I had to take a break from attempting a relationship with him.

Amidst everything with my parents—their disapproval, the discomfort I felt being around them, rectifying a relationship with Mom, and maintaining relational distance from Dad—I desperately wanted them to support me on this new journey of adulthood. I wanted them to understand that I wasn't trying to be disobedient in my choices (a frequent statement my parents had made). I remembered what the Apostle Paul wrote about obedience in Ephesians 6:1-3 (NLT), which says,

"Children, obey your parents because you belong to the Lord, for this is the right thing to do. 'Honor your father and mother.' This is the first commandment with a promise. If you honor your father and mother, 'things will go well for you, and you will have a long life on earth.'"

I knew this commandment well (as it is one of the Ten) and desired the promise of having a good, blessed life. Since I was an adult making my own choices, I didn't believe I had been disobedient, but my parents thought otherwise. I began to contemplate how to apply this scripture to my circumstances.

In my analysis of these verses, I discovered that honoring my parents isn't strictly an act of obedience but an expression of *respect.* Since I was now an adult and no longer under their direct authority, I could honor them through my actions and integrity. I respected my parents through my attitude, expressing love, honor, and grace whenever possible (instead of holding onto resentment and anger). I knew my actions in respecting my parents wouldn't be perfect, but I recognized that the value was in my effort to try, and that was my goal. Even though I still held onto a lot of hurt from their disapproval, I tried to do my best to honor them, a lesson that took many years to understand and still needs to be practiced on occasion. The reality that obedience isn't the only action that shows respect to one's parents has released another portion of the mantle's control in my life.

In the fall of 2010, Jon and I began the most dreaded moment of any dating relationship: *long distance.* At the time of our high school graduations, we had been dating for four years. We had spent every waking moment together and became practically attached at the hip; we were obsessed with being together.[2] However, as we began making plans for our future after high school—me praying my heart out to know God's will and Jon earnestly applying to university engineering programs—we recognized the importance of pursuing our own careers and becoming our own persons. The thought of being away from each other was terrifying, especially to my codependent self, but we felt like this was something we had to do for the growth of our own identities. So, as I packed up my life

---

2. A huge "thank you!!" is overdue to each of our parents for the sacrifices they made to allow us constant time together.

to live with Gram, Jon also packed up his life and began his four-year degree at Penn State University.

Our first year of long distance was excruciating. We talked every day and texted as often as we breathed, but it still wasn't the same. After the first few weeks, I was convinced we should break up; maintaining a long-distance relationship was just too hard. We needed to be present in our lives, not distracted by each other, and I wasn't sure how we could possibly find that balance. If I'm honest, I didn't know how to cope without Jon. He had become a safe space in the chaos of my world and being apart felt like pure torture.

When I suggested that we break up, Jon wouldn't hear of it. He believed we could survive the trials of long-distance (it hadn't even been a month yet!). At my opposition, Jon left his dorm room and found an empty meeting room for more privacy, spending several hours over the phone advocating for our relationship. I didn't want to break up with Jon; he meant everything to me. I just didn't know how we could make the distance work. Jon believed that long distance wasn't a reason to break up. We had already invested so much into our relationship that it deserved a chance to try to survive the distance. Jon believed in us, and amidst my worries, I chose to trust in his confidence.

To help our transition, Jon and I created routines to connect with each other and cope with the distance. We designated certain times for regular communication—morning wake-up texts so we knew the other was alive and ready for class on time and bedtime calls so we could spend the last moments of our day talking to each other. We texted or called each other during any free moment from our work and class schedules. Jon and I also prioritized seeing each other in person every two weeks, which happened more often than not. The distance wasn't ideal, but we made every effort to invest in our relationship and make it work.

◆—● ●—◆

While Jon was away beginning his engineering degree, I enrolled in the early childhood program at a community college. As I settled into classes, I quickly realized that my struggles throughout grade school weren't because of my academic stupidity; I was actually quite smart. I excelled in both prerequisite courses and early childhood classes, even rising to the top of my class in the math section I was taking.

After my third semester, I was inducted into the Phi Theta Kappa honor society for my 4.0 GPA. The college held a formal ceremony to honor each inductee adorned with a stole and gown, an event filled with pride and prestige. It was a surreal experience to achieve such a distinguished grade point average and receive the honor of being in an elite society. I couldn't believe that this was my reality! It felt like something I didn't deserve, yet I had earned it. My ability to work hard and attain academic success made me realize I was smart and worthy after all.

As I continued to excel in college, I began considering what I wanted to accomplish with a degree in education.

What did I want to teach?

Where did I want to teach?

With these questions came the option of transferring to a university program. At community college, I would earn an associate degree, opening the door to work in early childhood settings such as preschools and childcare centers. However, with a bachelor's degree from a university, I would have all the credentials necessary to apply for state certification and teach anywhere within my grade-level specialty. Before I continued with my current degree, possibly wasting time and money if courses didn't transfer toward my desired major at a university, I needed to decide which career direction I wanted to pursue.

Ultimately, my desire to attend university and become an elementary teacher swelled within my heart. Without delay, I began applying to four-year education programs throughout the area. I received acceptance letters from all six universities I applied to, and my weekends soon were packed with campus visits (and calls with Jon dispersed in between). I planned to visit every school I was accepted to compare their education programs, tuition costs, campus size, and distance from home. A detailed pros and cons list was essential!

While preparing for my college transition, it was important to me that my mom be a part of the process. We had spent the last year improving our relationship, and I wanted to include her in this next chapter. She was becoming my friend again, and I thought this would help redeem some of the hurt caused by our post-graduation disagreement. I wanted to allow my mom to support me and watch God's plan for my life unfold.

I invited Mom to join me and Gram on a campus tour of Slippery Rock University, a local state school known for its excellent education program.[3] This visit was specifically for transfer students who were pursuing college degrees and wanted to transition their educational efforts to SRU's esteemed programs.

---

3. Fun Fact: Dr. Phil once alluded to Slippery Rock in an interview as a fictitious school. He was quite surprised when the Rock Nation community proudly announced his inaccuracy, to which he humbly apologized.

Our visit started with all attendees assembled in the University Union building where we signed in, grabbed our information packets, and separated into groups based on our field of study. Mom, Gram, and I located the group of teaching prospects and waited for the education department presentation to begin. I don't remember anything about the presentation, but I can still feel the hope that was bouncing inside my gut as I silently prayed for clear insight. Something inside of me buzzed with excitement about being at Slippery Rock.

At the conclusion of our visit, we were given a campus tour. Our tour guide graciously answered questions while pointing out important spots on campus, like the new Robert M. Smith Student Center, Boozel Dining Hall, Bailey Library, and McKay Education Building. As our group strolled through the quad, I noticed the prominent boulder in its center, known for its magical powers when rubbed for good luck before an exam. As I stared at the large rock, a peace that surpasses all understanding filled my heart (Philippians 4:7). Before the tour was over, I knew that I was going to transfer to Slippery Rock. *This was where I was meant to become a teacher.*

In the fall of 2012, after three successful semesters at community college and almost two years of invaluable experience working in childcare, I ventured away from my comfort zone and leaped into the social menagerie of university life.

Choosing to attend SRU was a no-brainer. Only an hour away from home, with under 10,000 students, a quaint campus, and their recognized education program, I knew that my dream of becoming an elementary teacher could come true.

My time at Slippery Rock was indescribable! The things I learned, the friends I made, and the experiences I had were opportunities that unlocked a whole new perspective of self-worth and validation in my life. As I advanced in my studies and achieved academic goals, I became obsessed with my work ethic, striving to be a competent, dependable, and studious undergraduate. The value I had removed from the mantle's clutch was now attached to my calling to become a teacher, and I believed that was where I'd find my true identity. I knew that the Lord destined me to work with kids and that becoming an elementary teacher was His purpose for my life. I saw God's hand of blessing throughout my transition to college and the unimaginable academic achievements I was gaining. I felt valued, favored, and privileged for all that I was doing to obtain my teaching degree. This was the beginning of my *destiny*.

The end of my first semester at Slippery Rock meant one thing: Christmas break! I was excited to come home and celebrate all the traditions of the holiday season, but I was most looking forward to spending three whole weeks with Jon. A break from long distance was a present in itself!

Since we first started dating, our parents requested uninterrupted family time during holidays, leaving us to celebrate Christmas together on a different day. Our sixth-month anniversary is mid-December, so Jon and I designated that day as our special Christmas. This year was our six-and-a-half-year anniversary, and Jon wanted to plan the day as part of my Christmas present from him. This wasn't an unusual request coming from my thoughtful boyfriend, but I did speculate about his intentions.

Over the last several months, Jon and I had discussed the prospect of marriage more often than usual. I shared this with a friend, and her excitement encouraged (a bit too much) my desperation for a proposal even more. I began to anticipate our engagement almost every weekend Jon and I were together (which drove Jon *insane!*). One weekend that fall, we were hiking a nature trail in North Park, and I was convinced this was our moment. But as we finished the walk, I realized Jon wasn't going to propose, and my heart sank. When we returned to the car, I got very emotional, upset that Jon didn't want to marry me (which wasn't true), and mad at myself for ruining this wonderful date with my engagement-crazy expectations. I was determined that next time, I wouldn't let my excitement get in the way of our quality time together. I'd wait for Jon to propose to me on his own time.

Christmas has always been a source of happiness throughout my life. In the magic of the season, I couldn't help but desperately wish for our Christmas day this year to lead to Jon's proposal. However, I didn't want to get carried away and ruin what Jon had worked so diligently to plan, so I pushed my hopes aside and focused on our special day together.

When Jon came to pick me up that Sunday morning, my stomach was full of fluttering butterflies. I knew we were going on a road trip adventure (one that required my passport), so I wasn't too surprised when Jon handed me a piece of paper with a decorative golden bow delicately placed in the corner detailing the MapQuest directions to our destination: *Niagara Falls, Ontario!*[4]

We spent the four-hour car ride blaring holiday tunes and current hits while we laughed and sang along together. The

---

4. This was before unlimited data plans and the Google Maps app.

day was overcast and breezy with a winter chill in the air. We spent the early afternoon walking near the Falls, observing its overpowering cascade of rushing water as seagulls flew above its rising mist. Later, we went to a few shops and toured the busy streets of the Clifton Hill district before our early dinner reservation at the Pinnacle Restaurant. The restaurant towered twenty-six stories above the street with a gorgeous panoramic view of the Falls from the large window adjacent to our table. After enjoying the most elegant meal we had ever eaten, we had one last stop before heading home—a ride on the Niagara SkyWheel.

The SkyWheel is a Ferris wheel in the middle of Clifton Hill, with views of the magnificent waterfalls from its enclosed passenger cars. In December, the Falls are lit up for Christmas with beams of green, yellow, red, and blue lights shining behind the plummeting water. As we settled into our private passenger car and the SkyWheel began rotating, Jon and I took in the magical views of the waterfalls below. Suddenly, I noticed Jon holding a small velvet box. My entire world fell silent. I tried to take it all in—the ambiance of the holiday-lit Niagara Falls against the black night sky and the loving sentiments my boyfriend was expressing to me—but I couldn't retain any of it. Excitement flooded my mind, the hope of finally becoming his fiancée potentially about to come true!

Just as my heart was about to skip a beat with delight, Jon opened the delicate box. Inside was a vintage diamond pendant. In a matter of nanoseconds, my heart fell. Jon explained that he had the pendant made from an old ring of my GG's, a sentimental gift that should've had me gushing in appreciation.[5] However, I couldn't help but feel disappointed that it

---

5. GG had passed away eleven years earlier and this was a special gift to honor her memory.

wasn't an engagement ring. Gently, I picked up my forlorn heart and tried to accept his gift with gratitude.

As I lifted my eyes to thank Jon for my present, I noticed he wasn't sitting beside me. I looked up and saw Jon on bended knee on the wobbly floor of our passenger car with an identical box in his hand, propped open with a gorgeous diamond and sapphire ring inside. In my astonishment, I heard Jon ask, "Rebecca Elizabeth, will you marry me?"

Instantly, I began sobbing. Emotions erupted inside of me like a fireworks display, all the wonder, excitement, and joy I felt having this moment finally happen! Through my tears, I asked, "Jon, what are you doing?", too paralyzed by the shock of his proposal to verbalize an appropriate response. Patiently, Jon told me that he was trying to propose to me, and he repeated his question. This time, I replied with a tear-filled and joyous, "Yes!"

Following Jon's epic proposal, the start of a new semester was soon upon us. Heading back to Slippery Rock was exciting, telling all my friends and classmates about my engagement and showing off my beautiful new ring. However, I needed to stay focused on my education degree.

Upon enrollment at SRU, I was able to transfer all my credits from community college and apply them toward my university major. My transfer credits mostly consisted of general education courses, but some substituted for a few core education classes. The acceptance of these credits meant that I could graduate in three years. However, I faced an unanticipated obstacle: a state certification exam called the PAPA.

The Pre-Service Academic Performance Assessment (PAPA) involved the successful completion of three basic skills modules: mathematics, reading, and writing. Before proceeding to the official college of education program, I had to pass the PAPA exam. This meant that if I was unable to achieve a proficient score on either module, I would not be admitted to the education department at SRU nor acquire a state teaching license, and thus would be unable to graduate with a teaching degree. I felt my entire future riding on this exam.

In preparation, I studied every topic covered and completed every studying material available to guarantee my victory over this standardized test. After my first attempt at the PAPA, I successfully conquered the reading and writing modules but did not triumph over the mathematics section. I felt embarrassed and completely discouraged. I had no choice but to continue studying and testing until I passed the math portion of the exam.

After several failed attempts, I participated in a tutoring program for the mathematics module. It was a real struggle for me to understand these math concepts because the test covered high school courses I had never taken, such as trigonometry and calculus, plus my brain just doesn't compute numbers very well. The support from my tutor was beneficial, but the effort to learn and solve such confusing equations was daunting. I took the PAPA mathematics module again and *failed*.

I remember sitting in one of my education classes in my third semester at SRU, listening to an inspiring story about a student and their educational success achieved with the support of an influential teacher, and I tried not to cry. I wanted to be a teacher who made a positive difference in their students' lives, but I never could if I didn't pass this stupid test!

Internally, I felt hopeless, disappointed in myself for failing at such a simple task (multiple times), confused by the passion I had to become a teacher and the fight I wasn't winning to make that dream a reality.

As I walked through the quad back to my dorm room, I prayed for the Lord's help amidst this overwhelming roadblock (and even rubbed the favored rock for good luck). I believed that God brought me to Slippery Rock to become a teacher, so only by His intervention would I be able to successfully pass the PAPA and move forward with my teaching degree.

It had almost been a year since I began this prolonged testing nightmare, and if I didn't pass the PAPA soon, I wouldn't be able to continue with my education major. During my last attempt at the mathematics module, I remember praying my way through the entire exam, inhaling the peace of God's promises, and exhaling every worry and fear. As the testing proctor handed me my final score, I couldn't believe it—I had *finally* passed the exam! I was overcome with relief, excitement, and gratitude. I *was* going to earn my teaching degree after all.

I spent the next two years immersed in the world of education, discovering different types of pedagogy, learning how to differentiate academic instruction, and understanding how to communicate effectively with students and families. I observed intentional teaching techniques from veteran educators and experienced hands-on training through field experience in several elementary classrooms. To say that my experience at Slippery Rock was invaluable is an understatement—it was *unbelievable.*

The most impactful experience I had during my undergraduate program occurred during my student teaching placement in my final semester of college. I was placed in a small, urban elementary school and was assigned to a lively class of twenty-one first graders. The classroom was filled with an atmosphere of warmth, acceptance, and collaboration. It was spacious and inviting, every piece of furniture situated in a precise place, each decoration tastefully positioned along the walls and atop cabinets, never feeling cluttered or overstimulating. It was a comfortable, clean, and safe place for each student to learn and thrive.

The classroom teacher, Mrs. Fritzley, exuded positive energy in every interaction she had with her students, whether she was bringing an instructional lesson to life, intently redirecting an off-task behavior, or reminding the class of their responsibility to show kindness and respect toward others. Through her intentional lesson planning, thoughtful consideration of each student's needs, and authentic rapport with the class, her passion emanated throughout the classroom. Being a part of her first-grade class and learning under her advisement and expertise was an inspiring experience as a novice teacher.

Throughout student teaching, Mrs. Fritzley scaffolded each classroom routine and lesson structure while I observed her flawless instruction. Gradually, she assigned subjects for me to teach independently until I became the solo teacher of every lesson and daily routine in her classroom.

Morning meeting was my favorite part of the day! It was a special opportunity to establish community amongst the class and build relationships with each student. We sang greeting songs, reviewed concepts, answered daily questions, and counted our school days. One morning, we were reviewing a lesson when I spontaneously decided to elaborate on the topic and have a comprehensive discussion with the class. Afterward, Mrs. Fritzley told me that she had considered interjecting to help expound upon student learning, but I had already taken the initiative to do so, and she was impressed. She commended my intuition to think ahead and extend the students' learning and mentioned how she admired the maturity of my teaching instincts as an inexperienced student teacher.

I'll never forget one math lesson I taught, the *median* and *mode* in a set of numbers. In preparation for the lesson, I was a bit confused about how to explain this concept to the students clearly. Describing how to align a set of data sequentially and locate the number directly in the middle as the *median*, and then identify the number that repeats the most amount of times in the data set as the *mode* was a lot of information for students to process. The concept made my own brain pirouette with confusion! However, the curriculum activity seemed simple enough, so I felt comfortable instructing in the moment rather than planning ahead.

During lunch, Mrs. Fritzley asked if I was prepared for the math lesson to follow. She mentioned the number line for the activity, and I told her that I thought I could create it as I instructed. However, she advised that it must be ready beforehand, so I scarfed down my salad and sprinted back to the classroom before Mrs. Fritzley returned with the students. I haphazardly ripped off a long slice of butcher paper and crookedly scribbled numbers and dash lines to represent a number line. Luckily, I got the number line ready just in time; however, my explanation of the concept was far from polished. Mrs. Fritzley effortlessly interrupted the lesson to help support my instruction, knowing just what to say and how to describe the information to assist each student's understanding of the concept. I felt embarrassed not being properly prepared for the activity. Still, I was immensely grateful for Mrs. Fritzley's gracious guidance and effective support to help me learn and grow from my mistakes.

Being assigned to student-teach with Mrs. Fritzley was one of the best opportunities I was granted at SRU. I am forever grateful for the experience and her frequent encouragement which helped mold me into a more thoughtful, intentional, and considerate educator. Mrs. Fritzley has been a constant support throughout my teaching career.[6] I owe much of my talent and success to the lessons I learned as a novice teacher under her supervision and guidance.

My commencement from Slippery Rock was held on a sunny (and abnormally humid) Saturday in May 2015. The whole day was surreal; I couldn't believe I actually earned a bachelor's degree. What was even more impressive was that every semester, I had received Dean's List distinction, and I was graduating with *summa cum laude* honors with a 3.9 GPA![7] Never in my wildest dreams did I imagine my academic journey being this blessed.

My graduation was a whole family affair with my parents, brothers, Gram, and Jon attending, along with Jon's parents and his sister, Sarah. I was overwhelmed with appreciation for everyone who came to support me. In a way, my graduation was a redeeming moment in my relationship with my parents. When I began my journey toward teaching, my mom and dad were unsupportive and disapproving of my plans, but now they were *there*, watching my plans become a reality. From the beginning, all I wanted was for my parents to understand

---

6. And a cherished friend for almost a decade.
7. Not a 4.0 GPA because of the B I received in an online Meteorology course, but I digress.

God's will for my life, and as I succeeded along my college path, they finally realized that this was God's plan for my future. I may not have executed my choices perfectly, but there was no doubt that the Lord had called me to become a teacher, and everyone who came to celebrate my graduation agreed.

Before the ceremony, my family entourage walked around campus with me, stopping at all the major sights to take pictures of me in my cap and gown.[8] When we reached Morrow Field House (the location of commencement), sweaty and in desperate need of the comforts of air conditioning, it was time for the graduates to arrive and prepare for the processional.

I don't remember the specifics of the ceremony, how long it lasted, who the commencement speaker was, or what any presenter even said. But I do remember simply being in awe of the moment. I couldn't believe I was sitting at my college graduation, about to receive a degree in early childhood education and become a teacher! I held my name card in my hands—checking a dozen times that my name was spelled legibly and my major was labeled correctly—waiting to cross the platform, claim my diploma, and flip my tassel toward my future ahead.

As I reflect on my college career, I'm amazed by the Lord's favor. How did a naïve little girl raised in a dysfunctional household with a clumsy academic foundation excel through student teaching, obtain a bachelor's degree, and graduate with highest honors? Only by the goodness of God's grace and mercy did He equip me to accomplish this unimaginable dream and begin my career. This time taught me that when God calls you toward a purpose, He will make a way through every adversity for your success and His glory!

---

8. Of course, I got a picture sitting proudly on top of the quad's Good Luck Boulder!

—————

Six weeks after I graduated, another adventure was about to begin—*marriage!* Jon and I were engaged for two and a half years before our wedding, taking our time to complete our college degrees before jumping into married life. Planning preparations were well-dispersed during summer breaks, but things got much busier once my senior year started and our wedding date inched closer. It was overwhelming to balance my school schedule, graduation requirements, long-distance, and wedding details all at once! By the time our thirty-day countdown began, I wished we had just eloped (not really, but the stress was that intense).

Thankfully, our families were eager to help with our wedding planning needs. Whether we needed to track down addresses of second cousins or missing RSVPs, organize table place cards or sort through old photos, book a last-minute videographer, or pay for our wedding photographer, our families were ready to lend a helping hand. However, Jon and I had to make some difficult decisions, specifically about whether to include my dad.[9] My relationship with Dad had been a rollercoaster of hills, dips, and sharp turns, and I wasn't sure if I wanted him to be a part of such a special day in my life. However, I knew my wedding was an important time to honor my dad, so Jon and I included him, adapting a few things to respect his role in my life.

Finally, our wedding day arrived in June 2015. The day was a literal *dream,* with every detail falling into impeccable place. The weather was slightly overcast, creating the best

---

9. At one point during our engagement, I didn't even know if I would *invite* Dad, let alone include him.

lighting for gorgeous photos, and it only drizzled before the ceremony, leaving the rest of the day perfectly clear. I felt exquisite that day—my dress fitting just right, my hair laying just so, the true love beating in my heart from our nine years of devotion. My long-awaited, dream-come-true wedding day was finally here! I literally couldn't have been happier.

It was important to Jon and me that we dedicate our wedding day and the beginning of our marriage to the Lord.[10] We believed that He destined us for each other, and we knew that God had sustained our relationship throughout high school and the chaos of long distance during college. He was the reason we were together, and we wanted the Lord's continued favor to be upon this new chapter of our lives.

Before the ceremony began, Jon's Uncle Matt (our officiant) prayed over us and our marriage. As Jon and I held hands (separated by an open door so Jon couldn't see me), we felt an emotional calm settle over us. Uncle Matt described the atmosphere as *holy ground*, a sacred moment in the Lord's presence. This time of prayer was special, an important start to the rest of our lives.

Afterward, my walk down the aisle was just as emotional. The reality that I was about to marry the love of my life felt surreal. As my last bridesmaid made her entrance, my Uncle Jon squeezed my arm and gave me a loving wink, reassuring me of his support.[11]

Our wedding ceremony was held at a historic Methodist church on the North Side of downtown Pittsburgh. It had

---

10. Just as we had desired Christ to be at the center of our relationship almost a decade earlier.

11. Uncle Jon is my Aunt Emily's husband. He graciously agreed to escort me halfway down the aisle to Jon (my groom) so that he could see me for the first time during the processional. (Who knew talking about two people with the same name could be so confusing!)

elegant stained-glass windows and vintage wooden pews (with original cushions!). Toward the back of the sanctuary, two aisles intersected to create a break in the seating arrangement, sectioning off rows into defined groups of several pews. When the doors into the sanctuary opened, and everyone in attendance rose for my grand entrance, Jon was waiting at the aisle intersection, ready for the first look of his beautiful bride. When Uncle Jon and I reached the middle of the aisle, he gave Jon a firm handshake, taking my hand from his arm and placing it onto my groom's, and Jon and I finished the processional together.

When we reached the altar, Jon and I parted ways to greet our parents, each pair awaiting our acknowledgment. After we embraced them and exchanged loving sentiments, Jon and I rejoined for the giving of the bride as my parents proclaimed, "We do," in approving unison.

Our ceremony was short and sweet, yet it had so many specialized elements that made it perfect—like Uncle Matt's message about true love, a slideshow of pictures from our nine-year-long relationship during our unity sand ceremony, and the personalized vows Jon and I shared with each other. Standing in the presence of so much support, surrounded by all those whom we loved as we became husband and wife, was incredible. Throughout the ceremony, I may have felt rather overheated by the lack of air conditioning, desperately swaying to find the fan's breeze, and Jon may have been overcome with so much emotion that he barely smiled. Still, one thing was certain: this was the best day of our lives.

During our reception, Jon's Auntie Amy said the prayer over dinner. Before she prayed, she mentioned how priceless this day was—the ceremony, our relationship, the marriage we were about to begin. Her words were so true; everything about our wedding was *priceless*. The abounding grace of Christ radiated throughout every moment, His faithfulness to bring our relationship full circle as we became husband and wife. God's goodness overflowed on our wedding day, surpassing all I ever dreamed it could be. I never thought I deserved this much love or blessing. Through my wedding, the Lord redeemed parts of my life, those insecurities of shame and worthlessness, my past trauma upholding the mantle's atonement, and the conflicts between my parents and me. He lifted these burdens through the blessing of my marriage. My wedding day wasn't special because of anything I did to deserve it but because God wanted to use this moment to redeem my life for *good*.

In addition to my marriage vows, I committed to living with my husband (*obviously*), which meant moving away from Pittsburgh. After Jon graduated from Penn State University in 2014, he acquired an engineering job with General Motors, headquartered outside of Detroit. Thus, our marriage was destined to begin in the beautiful state of *Pure Michigan*.

I felt a lot of emotions during that time of transition—excitement to finally be married and start our life together, nervousness about moving away from the comfort of home, apprehension about being in a new place and finding my niche, and sadness as I was so far away from our friends and family. Yet, I felt immense happiness partnering with my husband in this exhilarating adventure of life! I didn't know what to expect with all the changes, but I knew that with Jon's love and support, everything would be all right.

As Jon and I began married life, we quickly noticed how our family influences affected our marriage. I was a bit jealous of (yet very grateful for) the positive examples Jon had in his family that modeled supportive and loving marriages. During our dating years, I spent some time with Jon's extended family at birthday parties, regular Sunday lunches, and summer barbeques. At one family gathering, Jon's married aunts and uncles congregated together, conversing and laughing while their children played in the next room. One of Jon's aunts had gotten up from the couch, and before leaving the room, she bent down to hug her husband. As she stooped down to embrace him, Jon's uncle placed his hands across her back and went in for a kiss! All the adults giggled at their affection, jokingly saying, "Maybe you should get a room!" while I sat nearby, awestruck by the situation. Their interaction was lovingly innocent, not inappropriate in the slightest, but it wasn't something I was used to observing. Watching married couples interact so infatuated with their spouses was a foreign expression of love from my perspective.

As for my family's influence, the impact wasn't as lovingly supportive. Developmental psychologist Gordon Neufeld explains that "children do not experience our intentions, no matter how heartfelt. They experience what we manifest in tone and behavior."[12] Even though my parents had good intentions to raise me well, their constant fighting affected the development of my learned behaviors. I'm ashamed to admit that I carried my parents' damaging habits into my own marriage.

Jon has *never* deliberately hurt, belittled, or demeaned me, ever. He has always shown me the most overwhelming care

---

12. Gabor Maté and Gordon Neufeld, *Hold on to Your Kids: Why Parents Need to Matter More Than Peers* (Random House, 2019).

and unconditional devotion imaginable; he epitomizes sacrificial love. Unfortunately, whenever conflicts arose throughout our relationship, I would resort to the tactics I observed from my parents—yell, cry, humiliate, and criticize. Even though I had utilized these strategies throughout many arguments in our nine years of dating, it wasn't until our first "fight" as a married couple that I realized the significance of my prior learned behavior.[13]

I don't remember what sparked this precise conflict between my husband and me, but I know my mental lid entirely flipped. Due to my perfectionism, I've always struggled with managing conflicts and handling confrontation. Whenever I've faced these circumstances, I often fight, fly, or freeze.[14] During this particular argument, I chose flight and marched upstairs to escape Jon's presence. I needed to get away from the strain of our disagreement and relieve the tension suffocating me. However, Jon followed right behind me as I ascended the stairs, hoping to calm me down and rationally discuss the matter that erupted between us. His pursuit made my blood boil—*why couldn't he just leave me alone?!*[15]

I don't recall what was said between us, but I know that I was screaming (and probably crying) and using heartless language. I tried to sneak into the guest bedroom before Jon reached the upstairs landing, but I wasn't quick enough. Jon pushed the bedroom door open as I tried to close it, imploring me to talk to him while I paced the room. Suddenly, I felt an urge deep inside my gut convincing me to do something

---

13. I use the term "fight" lightly because I was the only one reacting out of frustration.
14. Remember those terms from Psychology 101? They're real.
15. Jon's pursuit subconsciously triggered past instances where Dad would chase Mom upstairs, yelling terrible things at her. Although my husband wasn't yelling at me, the experience was identical to my traumatic memory.

destructive. In a matter of seconds, I wriggled my wedding ring off my finger and deliberately threw it across the room. The very symbol of my marriage's love and commitment, I tossed it into the air like it weighed nothing of importance. And the worst part is that I knew in my heart that it would hurt my husband. I chose to purposefully hurt the one person I love more than anything on this earth, the man who has only ever shown me true, unconditional love. I chose to hurt him because that's what I had learned to do during conflict.

I will forever feel humiliated and embarrassed by my actions that day. It was one of the worst decisions I've ever made, reacting in such hostility simply because it was a learned impulse. Seeing the hurt in Jon's eyes made me realize the significance of my actions. Whenever my lid flips during conflicts, the anger rising in me becomes so powerful that it overrides my brain and takes control of my reactions, and I physically cannot regulate my impulses. In those moments, I now know that I need to find safety, a mental space where I can de-escalate from the emotional chaos. After that "fight," I realized that my learned behaviors could not be an excuse for my current behavior; I needed to correct these habits before the patterns of my parents' marriage continued.

It took *years* for me to develop healthy ways to express my stress and anger during conflicts. The most beneficial strategy has been talking through my outbursts with Jon when I'm calm and regulated. He tells me how my yelling made him feel, and I explain what triggered my emotional explosion. Open and honest communication has been the key to helping me identify the importance of having time to de-escalate from triggers, and it has helped Jon understand how to support me best and when to approach resolution. It has also been eye-opening for me to realize that people can have arguments that don't involve shouting; people can disagree and still discuss things rationally.

About two years ago, Jon unintentionally upset me by stating (numerous times) how our taste in movies is so drastically different.[16] After hearing it for the umpteenth time (probably the third repetition), my mental lid flew open, and I marched upstairs. However, instead of yelling at my husband for making me upset, I shouted my feelings and (loudly) expressed the reason I was leaving: "It's my fault we can't pick a movie because I'm so difficult."

Although my reaction was a bit dramatic and irrational—I had blamed myself because I'm *still* healing from the insecurities of the mantle's standard of excellence—I chose not to entirely explode and spew my hurt onto my husband. Likewise, Jon left me alone to recover from the emotional stimulation instead of initiating an immediate resolution, letting me regain my composure before coming to check in on me.

Learning to correct my prior learned behaviors is a continual process, requiring much patience, diligence, and sacrifice from both Jon and me. I am indebted to my husband for his overwhelming grace and understanding as I continue to deal with and heal from my past trauma. His unconditional love and forgiveness have made all the difference for me to pursue a healthy, restored future. As I continue to rectify my learned behaviors, I'm grateful that my habit of yelling is diminishing. Although I may be tempted to raise my voice in moments of dysregulation, it's no longer a natural impulse. That is a sign of healing and progress in my life, and for that, Jon and I are grateful.

---

16. I didn't know it at the time, but I recently realized that there's something about the word *"drastic"* that triggers me. It makes me feel like I'm doing something wrong.

Despite the embarrassment and disappointment that I feel about that terrible first "fight," I have a sense of appreciation in realizing that the dysfunctional behaviors I witnessed during my childhood are not an excuse for my conduct now as an adult. I've chosen to look straight into the dark, nasty eyes of my problems—full of pain, shame, disgust, and fear—and fight for the healing and restoration I have craved for so long. With the Lord's help, I know these cycles will continue to dissolve in my life.

During my first year of married life, my parents decided to divorce. After twenty-five years of marriage, my mom and dad were finally ready to end the toxicity of their partnership and pursue healthier lives without each other.

When I found out about their decision, I was relieved. I never believed that my parents should have been together in the first place, not since I was a little girl and cried over their frequent discord. I knew that a divorce was in both my parents' best interests. However, as I digested the news, I began reflecting on my childhood and all the years that their marriage caused me distress. My memory took me back to the tension, the fights, the instability, the insecurity, and the dysfunction that surrounded my upbringing.

Amidst my grief, I went to Scripture to seek consolation. I came across Colossians 3:13, where the Apostle Paul says: "Bear with each other and forgive one another if any of you has a grievance against someone. Forgive as the Lord forgave you." I did have grievances against my parents for their hurtful actions that caused emotional damage in my life. I didn't want to forgive them for those mistakes. Yet, I knew I was supposed to bear with them and forgive. The last part of the verse that says, "Forgive as the Lord forgave you," was hard to accept because I knew how much grace God had given me. He had taken every sin, failure, heartbreak, mistake, and flaw in my life, wiped each imperfection as white as snow, and redeemed it all for *good*. I realized that I must forgive because Christ has graciously forgiven me.

That summer of 2016, I wrote this journal entry about my forgiveness journey:

"Oh Lord, I wish you could physically hold me right now. I'm so hurt and upset. I don't want to deal with this. I don't want to forgive my parents; it's too hard. I feel like I've separated who I was (my childhood) from who I am (adulthood). It's made it easier to deal with tolerating and respecting my parents. In my mind, seeing my little, innocent self and remembering things that happened— the fighting, yelling, attitudes, facial expressions, my inner concerned feelings—it makes me angry that they let those experiences happen so often to that little girl. They damaged her. They hurt her. They made it difficult for her to accept love and love herself. How selfish they were! That little girl didn't deserve to grow up that way and struggle through the internal challenges she's faced for twenty-four years. I used to be mad that they did this in front of my brothers, but now I realize the damage it did to me."

Processing the pain from my past trauma felt like internal torture. I couldn't wrap my head around it, let alone find clarity or peace. Even though I had been maintaining a relationship with my mom and tried working through things with my dad, I hadn't confronted the root of my heartache. Until I acknowledged the extent of my trauma, I would never experience true forgiveness toward my parents nor obtain freedom within my fragile soul.

I began to discover what true forgiveness meant to me. Previously, I thought forgiveness was like an official destination of sorts, a state of mind and heart where you arrived—after much turbulence out at sea—and were stationed there permanently. When the shore of forgiveness was reached, the anchor secured in its harbor, all that mattered was your arrival while every offense and hurt drifted away in the waves of your past. I was reluctant about this idea of forgiveness, the expectation that I had to let go and forget all the trouble that had defined my childhood and molded me into the person I became. As I contemplated this viewpoint, I realized that the significance of forgiveness isn't in the forgetting but in the *accepting*.

I believe that forgiveness is both a choice and a process. I don't forgive to forget what happened but to accept it and move forward. Some hurts will never be forgotten, but that doesn't mean they can't be *forgiven*. The act of forgiveness doesn't erase the past or exempt offenders from hurtful actions; it motivates us to reframe our attitudes, heal our heartaches, and restore our futures. Forgiving is how we take care of ourselves. When we look inside and deal with the effects of our past experiences, we open the door for restoration. The beauty of true forgiveness is the continual choice to face the difficult parts and keep moving forward, not letting the bad define us but using it to mold us into better people.

Forgiving my mom has been a fairly straightforward journey. The work we both did back in 2011 to communicate, apologize, and rectify our relationship greatly impacted our reconciliation. Watching her place herself in uncomfortable situations to prioritize me and support my decisions meant the world to me. I think we both learned a lot during those years of disagreement, and our relationship is better for it.

Since then, Mom has been a constant presence in my life, celebrating my wins and supporting me through hardships. Although our relationship has positively improved, I can still feel the hurt from my past. That's why there's compassion in forgiveness, to keep moving forward and sustain healthy relationships but still allow room to feel through the heartbreak and disappointment. The key to forgiveness is moving forward, and that's what Mom and I are striving to do. The past will always be a part of our story, but it will not define our present-day friendship. I love my mom and am grateful to call her *my friend* again.

Unfortunately, forgiving my dad and reconciling our relationship has been much harder. In 2021, I read Lysa TerKeurst's book *Forgiving What You Can't Forget* to help me fully process true forgiveness, especially toward Dad. Like an epiphany, I immediately recognized the abundance of anger, hurt, and frustration I still harbored toward him. I journaled this emotional entry around that time:

> *"I don't know why I have to go on this journey of forgiving my dad…When [Jon and I] got married, I tried so hard to do the right thing, forgive and move forward. [Dad] refuses to change, refuses to listen, refuses to be*

better, refuses to be selfless… I want nothing to do with someone who continuously hurts his family and doesn't work to make it better… I don't know if I'll ever forgive [Dad] completely…"

It was difficult to recognize how much emotional baggage I still carried from my dad's hurtful behavior, and I realized I needed to prioritize my well-being before forgiveness would ever be possible. That summer, I stopped communicating with my dad, no longer seeing him for holidays, responding to text messages, or staying in touch over social media. I'm sure these boundaries hurt my dad's heart, but they were necessary for my emotional health.

Despite my elimination of contact with Dad, he continued to reach out during holidays, birthdays, and our anniversaries. He respected my decision not to return communication, but it was important to him to still reach out and show care for his daughter (and son-in-law). Until I began writing this memoir, I hadn't reciprocated contact with Dad for nearly two and a half years.

Deep in my heart, I know my dad cares about me and desires reconciliation of our relationship. Honestly, this hiatus is the most I've ever felt loved and respected by my dad. These years of limited (or entirely ignored on my part) communication have rehabilitated my heart and given me the courage to try the forgiveness journey again. I don't know where our relationship will end up or if we'll ever completely reconcile, but I'm open to trying to forgive, and that's the first step.

Forgiveness has not been an easy lesson to learn, nor an effortless sacrifice to accept the hurtful memories of my past. Bandaging the wounds from my childhood, soothing the anxiety from such detrimental heartache, and watching each blemish become a delicate scar in my restored soul have brought peace and admiration for all that God has positively transformed in my life. Forgiving my parents has been another way I've experienced God's redemption. By taking something so profoundly devastating, the Lord has instilled a renewed spirit in me, creating a bright, positive, and healthy future.

As I've traveled this never-ending road of forgiveness, I've found comfort in the truth of Psalm 38:9 (NKJV), which says, "Lord, all my desire is before You; And my sighing is not hidden from You." God knows that my heart's desire is to forgive and respect my parents, and He knows how hard that process has been for me. God has heard my sighs of sorrow and distress in the journey. He cares about my emotional well-being, and He doesn't overlook the pain that I've gone through. He sees, He cares, He knows, and He will help me through every struggle.

In Matthew 11:28-29, Jesus told a crowd of followers, "'Come to me, all you who are weary and burdened, and I will give you rest. Take my yoke upon you and learn from me, for I am gentle and humble in heart, and you will find rest for your souls.'" I've also relied on this truth quite a bit in the forgiveness process. When I bring my burdens and weariness to Jesus, He teaches me with humility and gentleness, and by surrendering to God's will, my soul can find real rest. I can run to my Savior for endurance, compassion, and solace.

Forgiveness is not an easy lesson, but it brings so much freedom. Even though I will never forgive others perfectly, I know forgiveness is possible because the Lord has graciously forgiven me, and I can accomplish this task by the power of His strength within me (Ephesians 4:32; Philippians 4:13). The path of forgiveness has shown me that God's power is truly made perfect in human weakness (2 Corinthians 12:9).

Chapter Five

The Pursuit of Purpose

"I know that the experiences of our lives, when we let God use them, become the mysterious and perfect preparation for the work He will give us to do."

CORRIE TEN BOOM

You're God of the hills and valleys. One morning in the fall of 2022, this popular song by Tauren Wells came on my Spotify. The lyrics felt so personal, the promises within each line resonating like a peaceful breeze. After just surviving an exhausting "season in the valley," I felt grateful knowing God is sovereign over the hills in our highest moments *and* amidst the valleys of our darkest times.

And then I remembered. A year and a half prior, I had taught my first graders a social studies lesson about land formations (yes, I became a teacher—more on that later!). Each student selected a card with a particular land structure and used playdough to create a replica of that land formation: a mountain, plateau, plain, or hill. As the students got to work busily manipulating their playdough, joyfully conversing about their formations, and smudging their tiny fingerprints into the grooves of the dough, one student thoughtfully said, "Mrs. Kolenda, this reminds me of 'Hills and Valleys.' Can we listen to that song?" Any song by Tauren Wells was this group's anthem and praise. We frequently listened to his music while we ate snacks and completed projects, so of course I approved of the request.

I stood at the back of my classroom, watching my students create their land formations, listening to the sound of their sweet, innocent little voices singing these inspiring lyrics up to heaven:

> *"No matter what I have, Your grace is enough.*
> *No matter where I am, I'm standing in Your love."*
> *"You're God of the hills and valleys.*
> *And I am not alone."*[1]

---

1. Tauren Wells, *Hills and Valleys*. Album. USA: Provident Music Group, 2017.

My spirit soared with appreciation to the Lord. Right in the middle of an academic lesson, I was privileged enough to play worship music in my own classroom. Seeing my students learn and grow while including Jesus in every part of our school day was incredible. This was the unbelievable reality of my job, a dream I had longed to achieve.

That morning, while I reminisced of this precious memory and "Hills and Valleys" played throughout my bedroom, I lifted my hands toward heaven as tears of gratitude streamed down my face. The Lord had orchestrated everything in my life to lead me along this path of purpose. Twelve years earlier, I had no idea where my future would lead. I graduated high school full of unknowns. Now, I was experiencing the very future God had planned. I was overwhelmed by the Lord's faithfulness, realizing the impact He had destined me to achieve by becoming a *teacher*. Even if it didn't happen how I envisioned it, God was unfolding my destiny perfectly.

◄►━● ●━◄►

My teaching career didn't begin as effortlessly as I had hoped. After moving to Michigan as a fresh college graduate and newly certified educator, I was eager to start my profession and teach in my own classroom. However, I faced another hurdle in my teaching journey: Michigan certification. Even though I had a bachelor's degree in education and received my Pennsylvania teaching certificate, I was required to complete Michigan's testing requirements for state certification.[2] I was beyond frustrated with this reality, exhausted from the endless testing demands that seemed to hijack my attempts to become

---

2. Insert dramatic wailing, "WHY, GOD? WHY?"

a teacher. Didn't God see how difficult this was for me? How challenging academic exams were for me to overcome? Why did I have to face *more* testing after being so depleted already? Unfortunately, I had no choice. Jon's job was in Michigan, and if I wanted my own classroom, I had to follow state requirements and pass their exams. However unfair it seemed, this was my reality of becoming a teacher.

I began researching Michigan's teaching requirements and learned I could use my out-of-state license to teach for one year. After that time, I would be required to earn my Michigan certification. Hallelujah, testing could wait for twelve months! I knew that my mental endurance was shot from just completing college, and my emotional stamina was run ragged from the huge life changes of marriage and moving. Taking a break before attempting such rigorous testing again was essential.

When I began job hunting, I spent several days researching Michigan's educational system, learning how to obtain proper clearances, what reputable school districts were in my area, and how to apply for available teaching positions. I was delighted to find a local job fair recruiting teachers for open positions in Michigan's Great Start Readiness Program (GSRP) for preschoolers. GSRP provides a quality preschool education tuition-free to students primarily from low-income households. I've always appreciated the foundational skills taught during early childhood, and my stomach fluttered excitedly at the thought of becoming a preschool teacher! GSRP felt like the right opportunity for me to begin my teaching career.

As I prepped my resumé, I couldn't believe I was finally taking the first steps to begin my long-awaited dream career![3] At the job fair, I spoke with GSRP directors from various school

---

3. I even created a brochure all about me as an educator to set me apart from other teachers.

districts and privately owned childcare centers. As I introduced myself, explained my background, and beamed enthusiastically, I sensed an air of uncertainty with some of the directors. They seemed skeptical of my out-of-state certification and concerned about my lack of prior knowledge about the preschool program. However, I did my best to keep my worrying at bay, reminding myself that I was still a marketable educator.

One particular director was launching GSRP at her child-care center for the first year. Our conversation was comfortable and friendly. When she mentioned, "We'd be learning all this together," I sighed with relief. I've always valued a team mindset, and the idea of learning something new alongside others was reassuring. A few days later, the director contacted me for an interview, and within hours afterward, I accepted the position as lead teacher of her GSRP class. Dreams I'd longed for, worked diligently toward, prayed for, and believed for were actually coming true!

I spent the first three years of my teaching career teaching GSRP. The whole experience—where I worked, what I did, everything I learned—was an answered prayer, a defining opportunity to learn and grow as an educator. Having my own classroom and roster of students felt empowering, like I had finally defeated the forces trying to keep me from achieving my life's purpose. I told myself that I could now accomplish God's call on my life, constructing my identity around who I was meant to be as a teacher.

What I loved most about teaching preschool was seeing the extensive learning, discovering, growing, and exploring that young children naturally do in a supportive and nurturing environment. It took me back to my earlier days of babysitting and working in childcare. Sentimental memories of observing young children's play and discovering my love for the field of early childhood flooded my mind. I realized my passion for the care and education of little ones developed from my own childhood experiences. I wanted to be a loving, secure caretaker and teacher because I didn't have that support growing up. Even though my parents loved me and cared for me, I never felt emotionally safe in the dysfunction of our home. As an adult, whenever I watched young children thrive in healthy environments I worked in, it made me feel like my past was validated, as if I was making amends for the damaging circumstances that affected my own development.

Whenever I told people about my decision to become a teacher, they were often surprised that a homeschooled student would want to be an educator.[4] My desire to become a teacher wasn't just about teaching and instructing but also about caring and advocating for my students. Even though I was teaching in a different educational setting than I grew up in, I knew there were children there who needed an advocate, someone who would simply love and care for them on hard days, and I wanted to be that person.

I knew my first responsibility as a teacher was to my students' education. I valued the hands-on approach of preschool and my active role in facilitating learning through seemingly ordinary experiences. Through every play-based activity, I could find a way to reinforce language concepts, help them practice math skills, give them directions to follow, or provide

---

4. Some people assume that if you were homeschooled, you do not value the public education system.

tools for their physical development, like using safety scissors while cutting playdough to develop fine motor strength. Scaffolding learning through hands-on experiences was an essential practice of GSRP instruction.

One year, I had a student who adamantly did not want to learn how to put on his coat independently. Every time we went outside (especially during winter), he would pout, cry, kick his jacket across the floor, and refuse to put it on by himself. My teaching partner taught him a "trick"—placing his coat on the floor, standing above the hood, bending down and putting his arms through the sleeves, then raising the jacket directly above his head and flipping the coat over his back. *Voila!* Eventually, he caught onto this skill without much frustration, but zippering his coat was another battle to be won. This preschooler would wail, stubbornly sit on the ground, and refuse to attempt zippering it. With every sorrowful meltdown, I tried to meet him with patience, explaining that if he asked for help, we could zipper his coat together.

One spring day, after many months of this continual jacket-zippering fiasco, my student finally flipped on his jacket and zippered it up all on his own without shedding a tear! I was so proud of his independence, grateful that he had learned to do this simple skill without getting upset. The pride of his accomplishment beamed through his smile as he grinned from ear to ear. It was a sweet victory for his self-esteem and a special moment for me to witness his success.

Building relationships with my students was always a significant part of my job. Once, a preschooler told me, "I really wanted to come to school on Monday to see you," and another student said, "You're my best friend forever." These genuine comments of affection melted my heart into a puddle of endearment. From my experience, young learners often voice numerous expressions of *"I love you"* or *"You're my best friend"* when they feel loved, valued, and safe with someone. Hearing these sentiments from my own students meant they felt emotionally secure and cared for at school. I felt pleased knowing that I was creating a nurturing environment. It meant so much to me for my students to have a safe place where they felt comfortable learning new things and growing in their independence.

Time spent one-on-one with my students was special. Moments in our structured day when I neglected lesson plans to join their imaginative play were the most valuable ways I expressed my love and care for them. As I ventured into my students' play scenarios, I learned more about their personalities and quirks, admiring them as the incredible people they were becoming.

During my first year teaching, I had a preschooler who was obsessed with dune buggies and dirt bikes—really any vehicle that left the blacktop and went off-roading onto the grimy dirt or dusty sand. At recess one afternoon, my student shouted across the yard, "Miss Becca, come for a ride in my dune buggy with me!" I strolled toward the large tree he was sitting against, crouched down beside him, and adjusted my imaginary seatbelt as he began making loud steering and accelerating noises, indicating his impressive driving skills. I laughed and yelled along with him as we pretended to drive up sandhills and down bumpy dunes. Mesmerizing joy glistened in his eyes as his imagination took us on an off-roading adventure together.

Moments where I simply sat in the presence of my students' inquisitive minds were sacred. Observing the world through their innocent eyes inspired me as I realized that children's awe, wonder, and faith soon fade away when they grow up. As children become adults, they are often more critical, lack curiosity, and develop a mistrust of others. Even Jesus said, "Let the little children come to me, and do not hinder them, for the kingdom of heaven belongs to such as these," revealing the importance of a child's mindset (Matthew 19:14). Watching children grow and learning from their perspectives reminded me to appreciate the simple things in life. Early childhood is a unique time of life, and it was a privilege to be part of each student's journey of developing, learning, and growing. As much as I tried to teach them, they always taught me something new, too.

I enjoyed my first year of teaching GSRP, but testing for my Michigan teaching certification loomed overhead. I took the year provided with my Pennsylvania certification and acclimated to my new job, new home, and new life. However, once the next school year started, I knew I had to begin studying and testing again. Pennsylvania and Michigan had identical exams, which made it even more aggravating to have to take these tests *again*, yet no easier to pass.

Like my experience taking the PAPA, I conquered the reading and writing portion of the basic skills exam and failed the math section. *Here we go again.* Because I was teaching preschool full-time, I spent two years of holiday and summer breaks focused on retaking the exam, allowing myself time to study when school wasn't in session.[5]

Now, you should know that the Department of Education (at the national and local levels) is constantly changing, adjusting its protocols, guidelines, and requirements to better

---

5. Even though my temporary certification expired, I was able to keep my teaching position while I actively worked to pass the Michigan Test for Teacher Certification (MTTC).

suit whatever new and improved visions they have for the field. Due to the length of time between my testing attempts, I discovered that Michigan's Department of Education had eliminated the basic skills portion of the MTTC and replaced it with the universal SAT.

My blood boiled with fury at the realization that I was now required to pass the SAT (an exam that evaluates high school intelligence, not career capability)! It seemed like no matter how hard I tried, something kept preventing me from reaching my career goals, which was unbelievably frustrating. In my disparity, I couldn't help but think that if God wanted me to be a teacher, why wasn't He making the process easier? I thought my identity and life's purpose were supposed to be fulfilled through teaching. Despite my doubt, I knew the Lord would make a way. I had already overcome obstacles in my education journey and had to trust that my efforts were not in vain. I had to believe that the Lord would continue to be faithful.

Even so, it was humiliating sauntering into the local high school as a college graduate and certified teacher, completing the juvenile SAT alongside inexperienced, college-bound high schoolers. Fortunately, I received the minimum required score on the math section of the SAT and immediately applied for Michigan certification.

During preparation for the MTTC exam the previous summer of 2017, I journaled my hopes to the Lord, saying:

> *"As I go forward with further testing, in hopes of obtaining a teaching certification, in hopes of a grade-level position, I pray that you will lead and guide me—not just to the correct answers to pass the exam, but toward my purpose in life—let me be exactly where you need me to be."*

And when I finally applied for my Michigan teaching certificate in April 2018, I told God:

"Here I am, Lord. I passed all my exams, ready to become certified to do your will. Jesus, you have never failed me. Even when difficult things happen or preferred results aren't obtained, still you are faithful."

With my new teaching certificate in hand, I now had a decision to make: to continue teaching GSRP or pursue an elementary position. Although I loved early childhood and had felt called to be a preschool teacher, I believed the Lord was preparing a new chapter for my career. During student teaching, I fell in love with first-grade curricula, and the thought of using my expertise from that formative experience excited me!

Teaching in an elementary classroom seemed like the official stamp of a "real" certified teacher. To me, reaching that level of success meant that I finally achieved the highest standard of excellence for my career. The realization that my teaching title could now solidify my identity was exhilarating! However, more than anything else, I wanted to be where the Lord could use me to make a difference for my students. I still believed that my teaching endeavors were a part of His plan for my life, and with His continued guidance and blessing, I would be content to teach wherever He wanted me to.

Amidst the whirlwind of my decision process, I was introduced to the superintendent of a Christian K-12 school supported by the church Jon and I attended. Upon our chance encounter, he provided me with his business card and told me to send him my resumé, and he'd contact me about an interview for the following school year. My heart skipped a beat! This felt like the school I was supposed to teach at next.

◆—● ●—◆

The transition from preschool to private elementary education was bittersweet. I was saddened to leave my job— my first professional teaching experience and the early childhood field I'd grown so fond of. Yet, I felt such anticipation for what was ahead, another dream to come true!

Two elementary positions were open for the new school year: kindergarten and first grade. Although my interview placed me at the top of their candidate list, both positions were awarded to two other teachers with previous experience substitute teaching at the school. I was disappointed. That should've been my big break! However, the school planned to hire me for an assortment of roles that year, promising to consider me for a potential first-grade position the next school year.

I told myself I was content to be a versatile teacher—kindergarten aid by morning, elementary technology teacher by afternoon, and unexpectedly, an on-call substitute teacher any hour of the school day. I loved supporting others and thoroughly enjoyed learning from colleagues, so I believed I'd be satisfied during this year of untraditional teaching. However, a few weeks into the school year, I wrote this journal entry:

> *"God, I am struggling with my job position...I want to be better than this. I want to be more than this. I didn't go to college and fight through exams to be this...Did I? I love helping people and I know my flexibility and*

THE PURSUIT OF PURPOSE

willingness are a blessing to the school, but I don't feel like it's fulfilling my potential."

I was frustrated having just passed my second round of state certification exams, especially since the last one landed me back in high school. It felt like my talent and expertise were being overlooked, and I struggled with feelings of envy, resentment, and confusion. I wanted more than a fragmented position to be what I earned with my Michigan certification.

Through all the dissatisfaction I felt not having my own classroom, God reminded my heart of what really mattered— His purpose, His will, and His provision. I voiced my gratitude to the Lord in this journal entry, saying:

"Lord, thank you for speaking to me. Thank you for gently telling me what I need to hear in order to grow. I'm in anticipation for all you have in store as I continue this trusting journey with you. At the very end of worship Sunday, you spoke to me that I need to be a servant— pride comes before the fall (Proverbs 16:18). I've been very entitled about my degree and qualifications that I've been miserable in my position. I believe you are improving my servant heart; to be humble and not focus on what I 'deserve' or 'should have'... Thank you for correcting my spirit...Continue to grow me to meet my full potential."

It was a difficult pill to swallow, realizing I was too absorbed by my own achievements to acknowledge the opportunity I had to make a positive difference in the lives of my fellow coworkers and their students. I was embarrassed that I felt this position unworthy of my potential, even though I knew it was a privilege to serve others.[6] I had to accept that no matter what job I held, the Lord would use me to accomplish His will. And I had to learn that my identity and value weren't based on the title or position I achieved but on the obedience of my actions toward God's call on my life. Even though I didn't have my well-deserved classroom, I was still on the path toward reward and purpose.

As I processed this revelation, I journaled my appreciation of God's divine intervention, saying:

> *"Thank you for speaking to me. Thank you for telling me what I need to hear. Life isn't about me. It's all about YOU! Just because I have a teaching degree and state certification doesn't mean that's my goal and purpose. You directed me in that direction for your will. My life doesn't have to look like anyone else's. God has a perfect, unique plan for my life. May my human nature not get in the way of that."*

For most of that school year, I tried to support and serve my colleagues without selfish ambition. I truly cherished my position as a kindergarten aid and was grateful to have gained a friendship with the classroom teacher. We were both new to the school that year and confided in each other as we learned the ropes of different policies, new curricula, and classroom routines. As we developed a rapport, it was clear that our partnership was a match made in heaven. We found similarities in our life experiences, hobby interests, and moral beliefs. Every day was a fun time spent together in a room full of thirteen angelic kindergarteners.[7] I enjoyed being a source of

---

6. Even Jesus came not to be served, but to serve others (Mark 10:45).
7. No joke, it was the smallest, most well-behaved class ever.

encouragement and dependability for my friend, stepping in effortlessly when she needed a break, doing trite errands to the copier, perusing Teachers Pay Teachers for supplemental activities,[8] and being responsible for regular student assessments. Even though my role was minor, I felt my expertise was validated and appreciated. I never doubted the importance of my role as a kindergarten aid, and I valued the opportunity to observe and learn from an experienced educator like my friend.

However, this was not the only role I had that school year. I was also the technology teacher for kindergarten through third grade. This was an amusing position because I'm not technology savvy, plus the job description was non-existent, so I had to research state standards to teach appropriate content. The responsibility to create a structure for a position I didn't feel qualified for was unnerving (and rather stressful). I did my due diligence and appreciated gaining experience across grade levels, but I knew from the beginning that the technology role was not meant for me.

Additionally, I was also a substitute teacher. This unexpected role made me so apprehensive that a rash of red splotches would break out across my chest, ears, and face every time I was asked to sub. Each request instantly induced heat through my cheeks, the fiery sensation extending through my veins to the very tips of my ears. My heart raced at Olympic levels, my mind spinning in hopes of regulating the anxiety. Subbing spur of the moment went against my personality, as I was constantly pulled out of my regular routine and placed in an unfamiliar environment.[9] Although I had some apprehension about lower elementary requests, I did acclimate better to those substitute

---

8. An online marketplace of teacher-made classroom resources. It is an elementary teacher's saving grace!
9. My history of panic attacks and anxiety seemed to be caused by moments of change, where I lost control of my regular routines and had to adapt to new responsibilities.

days. It was upper elementary and secondary classes that made my stomach sink into Hades and catch on fire.

Amidst my anxiety, I diligently filled the need for substituting across the K-12 classrooms. However, my nerves never adapted to the uncertainty and distress I felt being responsible for older students and teaching unfamiliar curriculum. It was clear I was not created to be a substitute teacher, and I couldn't wait for a position change the next school year.

As the first signs of spring bloomed outside, I was adamant about receiving the first-grade position for the fall. However, my school had prolonged formalities before official approval could be confirmed. I was agitated by the uncertainty of the situation. I loved the religious fellowship among my coworkers, the guidance of biblical wisdom across school leadership, and the opportunity to include Jesus in every conversation I had with students. It was a privilege to be a part of a Christian environment, the freedom to live out my faith in the workplace. But as much as I enjoyed working at this school, I longed for my own classroom. I knew God had placed me in a role of servitude, but I struggled with feeling entitled to obtain a grade-level position as if that was confirmation of my purpose.

In desperation, I asked the Lord for wisdom. I believed that if God had put the desire in my heart to become a teacher, He would continue to be faithful. I had been (imperfectly) obedient to His will thus far, and I was finally ready for the Lord's plans to align with mine.

I searched for teaching vacancies, and a job fair popped up. I attended in hopes of job security in case the first-grade position fell through at my school. After the fair, I had several interviews, but none of the options felt quite right. Even though I tried to remain hopeful, doubt lurked around every corner as the school year proceeded and decisions were yet to be made. Finally, I was officially offered the first-grade position and immediately accepted it. I was overjoyed, relieved that God was finally opening the door I longed to walk through, providing me the teaching opportunity of my dreams!

◆— ● ●—◆

After a busy summer break in 2019, I journaled my gratitude to the Lord in preparation for the school year ahead:

> *"I cannot believe I have the privilege to teach first grade this year!!! I am so overwhelmed by your goodness, Lord. I cannot believe the blessings and important responsibilities you've given me. I'm so grateful to be used by you."*

And after the first week of school, I wrote:

> *"Lord, I am so happy to be teaching first grade. I've never felt so fulfilled! Thank you for calming my spirit and helping me through every challenge."*

Teaching first grade was a literal dream come true. My first class was especially unique because I knew each returning student from the technology class I taught the previous year. It was special to already have a rapport with most of my students as we began the year.

I was so excited about this new adventure that I created an adventurous theme throughout my classroom and took my students on a learning safari! I selected an assortment of safari décor for the perfect wildlife learning environment, the centerpiece of the classroom being a cardboard framework of a Jeep prominently secured to the front of my desk.[10] Jungle stuffed animals, artificial trees, safari Beanie Babies, and wildlife posters were scattered throughout my classroom to enhance our wild academic journey ahead. I even inducted each student into our safari adventure as a first-grade explorer.

Although there were some challenges to my new role, my students brought me such happiness. I remember one afternoon during lunchtime, several students spontaneously formed a conga line and erupted into a serenade of *"cha-cha-cha-cha-cha-CHA"* around the classroom! There was such joyful laughter in that moment, each student giggling whether they joined in the conga line or not. Watching my students have fun in a nurturing environment was all I ever wanted. As a little girl, I had found security at church, away from the emotional burdens of home, and now I was creating a safe place for my students. My classroom was a haven where they could learn, express themselves, and feel loved, no matter what.

After we moved to Michigan, Jon and I joined a local church and became involved with their young adult ministry. The group gathered every Sunday night, and during a service in February 2016, the directors of a foster care ministry came as guest speakers.

During the directors' presentation, they introduced Royal Family KIDS Camp (RFKC). RFKC is an international ministry supported by the church that provides one weeklong summer camp experience to children ages six through eleven

---

10. Designed and constructed by Jon!

growing up in the local foster care system.[11] The mission of RFKC is to create an uplifting environment to show the campers the love and grace of Christ while also turning fun moments into lasting memories. Over one hundred volunteers were needed to run the week of camp, and as I listened to the directors' call to action, I turned to Jon with tears in my eyes and simply said, "I have to do this." He tenderly smiled at me and said, "I know."

My emotional connection with children from hard places motivated me to become involved. Although I had been protected from the experiences of foster care, I had grown up in a dysfunctional home. I had undoubtedly experienced similar feelings of devastation that have impacted these children's lives, too.

The application process to volunteer with RFKC was extensive—to say the least! A formal application was required, along with three reference letters, a volunteer interview, a federal background check, and mandatory training hours. It seemed like a lot of formalities just to volunteer for a week of camp, but they are vital to ensure the protection of each camper. Working with the foster care system involves a lot of red tape, especially because RFKC is a religious program partnering with the state, and ensuring that every volunteer understands the legalities of the ministry is essential. Due to the varying backgrounds of the campers served, it is also important for directors to flag any potential volunteer who may not be safe or appropriate around young children.

During my interview, I was nervous sharing about my own childhood, concerned that it would prevent me from being accepted as a volunteer. I expressed my fears to Jon, already

---

11. The organization restructured in 2020 and is now called For the Children. Royal Family KIDS Camp is still an associated ministry within the organization.

attached to the idea of being a part of the ministry. I felt connected to RFKC's inspirational call to action, but my imperfect past made me feel unworthy of such a privilege. I could understand why I wouldn't be a good candidate because my background might be too similar to the campers'. I wondered if the directors would see past my brokenness and acknowledge my heart to serve. Hope and anticipation kept me on the edge of my seat until I finally received my volunteer acceptance letter. This was part of the Lord's will after all!

◄►─ ─ ─ ─◄►

At my first year of Royal Family KIDS Camp in 2016, I was assigned as a "walk along," a person who shadows a particular counselor pair to help supervise a camper with challenging behavior. My role also offered extra assistance to the counselors by providing them with momentary breaks, helping supervise routines for the entire cabin, and supporting transition times. Because I spent every moment "walking along" with their group, I built relationships with the counselors and their four campers, which was a special opportunity.

The camper I was assigned to help supervise required one-on-one attention. She wasn't always aware of her surroundings and frequently became distracted by little things in her environment. One time, when we were walking past a wooded area, something between the trees caught her eye, and she romped off. Her counselor reminded her to stay on the walking trail while both of us jogged into the woods right behind her.[12] What probably distracted her was a new spot to find

---

12. She didn't run too far and eventually turned around to walk on the trail with us. With her spontaneity, the counselors and I had to be ready at any moment to redirect her impulses.

rocks—she absolutely loved them! This camper would stop anywhere and everywhere along the campground to examine stones, selecting various smooth ones for her personal collection. On Water Blast Day, she didn't want to get wet in the sprinklers or slimy from the shaving cream-covered slip-n-slide, so she and I spent the entire time walking along the cobbled section of the building nearby, searching for the best stones to add to her camp rock collection. While we were exploring, one volunteer painted a stone into a ladybug for the camper to keep. The camper squealed with delight when she saw the decorated rock, excitedly grasping it from the volunteer's hand, turning it over in her own palm as she examined the artistry of red and black painted across the stone's smooth surface. Seeing the amazement light up in her eyes and watching a smile spread wide across her face was a moment I'll never forget.

My week at camp was truly life-changing. There aren't words to describe the awe-inspiring atmosphere within every breeze of the summer air while at camp. Observing the level of care from every volunteer, noticing how each person positively impacted the campers' experience was overwhelming. Although the campers are wards of the state, RFKC strategically follows appropriate state mandates to create a safe and appropriate environment for the children while never shying away from the gospel's message. The truth of Scripture is instilled into every camper's life through songs, Bible lessons, dramas, and personal conversations with the volunteers. Many people are skeptical that one week could make a difference, but I assure you, one week at Royal Family KIDS Camp made *all* the difference.

I came home exhausted yet beaming with pride. The more I reflected on my experience, the more I realized that RFKC was a new piece of my life's purpose. This was a new opportunity for me to work with children and help create safe, memorable, and fun experiences for these resilient, ambitious, and deserving campers. Volunteering with Royal Family KIDS Camp was something I was destined to do.

After camp, I learned that Royal Family KIDS (RFK) isn't just a weeklong summer camp; it also includes a mentorship program for the campers. The RFK mentoring club is a monthly event hosted during the school year that contains all the fundamental elements of the RFK camp experience but in a condensed, three-hour version. The volunteers needed to run the program include mentors to pair with each mentee (they spend about six hours every month together) and support staff who help run the monthly meetings. After such an inspiring week at camp, I knew I just had to be a part of club!

At the time, I was too nervous to be a mentor for a precious young girl, so I signed up for a support staff role. Although I could have committed the time to be a mentor, I found the idea of *me* being a role model absurd. I had absolutely no business being anyone's mentor, especially with my childhood experiences. I was a product of trauma, just like many of the children growing up in foster care, and even though I was now an adult able to make healthy life choices, I didn't feel competent to positively influence a young child's life. If the mantle's lasting impact taught me anything, it was that I would never measure up to being enough, and I knew *that* wasn't the kind of role model a little girl needed. All I wanted was to be involved with club, and I knew I could do that through a supportive role.

During our first club event in October, one of the mentees attended without her mentor. Seeing all the other mentees with their mentors must've been difficult for her because, during the middle of club, she went into the bathroom and locked herself in a stall. Different volunteers tried to entice her to rejoin the group, but she continued to sit stubbornly on the cold tiled floor, disinterested by each request. Instantly, I recognized her strong-willed attitude from our time together during camp.[13] One evening that summer, "E" (as I'll lovingly refer to her as) was playing on the playground when the transition to chapel was announced. As her counselor reiterated the message, E ignored every request and continued playing in the sandbox. Eventually, E took a few strides toward a nearby bench, plopped herself down, and refused to move further. Her counselor and a leadership team member sat for nearly fifteen minutes with E before she was ready to attend chapel.

After getting home from the first day of club, I told Jon about the situation with E in the bathroom and casually said, "I'll pray for her mentor." Not having her mentor at club was difficult for E, and I was worried about a successful mentorship. E deserved someone committed, and I didn't want her to go through the heartache of missing out on an important connection again.

A few days later, I received an unexpected phone call from the club director. She explained that E's assigned mentor could not commit to the mentorship that year, and she was curious if I'd be willing to step in. I was astonished by the request, hesitancy rising in my chest. I was relieved to be paired with a mentee I already knew, but a mentorship role was a huge responsibility. My mind swirled with doubt—*could I even be a*

---

13. She happened to be one of the campers in my cabin that previous summer.

good mentor? Despite the incessant negativity consuming my thoughts, I agreed with complete determination.

Being E's mentor was truly an amazing experience. E is an incredible person. She has an inquisitive mind to process things intricately, a thoughtful perspective that always enhances conversations, a loving care toward animals and her family, and an entertaining personality that brings fun to every situation. Of course, moments of headstrong behavior were inevitable, but I soon learned that as long as E's basic needs were met—food, water, rest, and security—she was ready to enjoy any adventure we had planned for the day.

Building a rapport with E felt easy, plus our common interests helped strengthen our mentorship as we both loved taking pictures, collecting stuffed animals, and going on adventures. It became a tradition for E to bring my personal Snoopy stuffed dog with us wherever we went—she'd even buckle him into his own seat during our car rides. My beloved Snoopy is captured in many of the photos documenting our adventures together, like our trip to the Detroit Zoo sitting with E on the elephant statue, at the SEA LIFE Aquarium watching the fish swim around while nestled tightly in E's arm, during a lunch date at Wendy's enjoying some fries with a napkin tucked underneath his chin, and at Three Cedars Farm where he helped E navigate the corn maze. Time spent with E created some of the most cherished moments of my life, and I wanted every event we went to and activity we did together to be a positive moment for her to cherish, too.

For Mother's Day, E and her foster mom made me a personalized acrostic poem using the letters in my name to describe the positive characteristics of my personality. E wrote at the bottom of the poem: "Thanks for being my mentor.

You are sort of like a mother to me, so happy Mother's Day." I cannot explain what that gift meant to me and how reading those words validated my role as a mentor. I had felt so inadequate to hold such an important role in E's life that my worries caused me to second-guess my value. I felt satisfied knowing that E was affirmed in our mentorship.

Although E and I spent quality time with just the two of us, Jon soon became a bonus to our adventures. One major rule of RFK club was not to be alone with your mentee, which wasn't a problem when we went out and about, but if I wanted to have E over to the house to bake cookies or do arts and crafts, I needed another adult to be present.[14] Luckily, Jon qualified as my "two deep," and E frequently came over to visit. E loved spending time with "Mr. Jon," and our activities felt even more special when he was there.

One summer day in 2017, E wanted to go fishing (Jon's long-lost but long-loved hobby), so I invited him to tag along with us for the day's excursion. The three of us set out for Kensington Park and rented a boat to enhance our fishing expedition. While Jon captained the rowboat and I sat utterly afraid we'd drown, E tried to fish to no avail. Jon steered us back to shore where he and E could fish more successfully, and I praised God for dry ground. As I watched Jon interact with E that day—being patient when she grew anxious waiting for a fish to bite, showing grace when E didn't want to touch the slimy, wriggly worms, guiding her cast into the perfect spot of the pond, or teaching her wise fisherman tips he'd learned as a boy—my heart was overcome with gratitude.[15] I appreciated

---

14. RFK has a standard "two-deep rule," which means there are always at least two trained adults with a child, never allowing them to be left alone or with only one adult present.
15. And immense adoration because whose heart doesn't flutter when their spouse shows genuine love and care toward others?

that E had the opportunity to build a special bond with Jon and had someone else to pour endless kindness into her life. Jon and I both felt privileged to know and care for E.

It sounds odd, but we saw ourselves in E—her spunky attitude and vivacious facial expressions were all me, and her intelligent mind and kindhearted soul were all Jon. We felt like if we had biological children, they would be like E. Whenever we spent time with her, our focus was never to pretend to be a functional family. We always respected the boundaries of mentee and mentor and loved E accordingly. Nevertheless, our connection with E was something special that Jon and I both treasured.

Before our mentorship, I may have self-sabotaged my belief in being an effective mentor, doubting my influence because of my broken past. But being E's mentor taught me that I don't have to be the perfect role model to make a difference; I just need a heart to love, care, and support a child. Most of our time together was spent having fun, enjoying a moment, and sharing the experience—not necessarily having intellectual conversations or discovering extraordinary revelations. We simply spent quality time together, and I think that's what makes a real connection in a relationship. It's by intention and consistency that we learn from each other, become comfortable, find our value, and know we are loved. Our mentorship also taught me that it's not just about the impact a mentor makes on their mentee but the bond they create between each other. E was only seven years old when I became her mentor, yet I learned so much from her positive and caring nature. I don't know how I measure up to other mentors, but I believe the Lord used me (and Jon) to bless E's life, and that's more than I could ever ask.

Unfortunately, as cases go in the instability of foster care, during my second year of mentorship with E, we learned that she was going to be moving away to live with a relative in hopes of possible adoption. In the blink of an eye, our mentorship was over. It was truly gut-wrenching losing our relationship with her. Our hearts were split in two saying goodbye to E, not knowing if we'd ever see her again. She was (and will always be) so special to both of us. I may have only mentored E for two years, but her lasting impact on our hearts will be with us forever.

⇥━ ━⇤

After my first year mentoring E, Jon decided to join RFKC— he "drank the Kool-Aid," as many veteran volunteers would say. My mentorship with E had developed a passion within our hearts to make a difference for children in foster care, and we both felt called to be a part of the ministry. [16]

In the summer of 2017, Jon and I decided to volunteer as counselors for camp. This was a much more demanding role than I had the previous summer, now partnering with a co-counselor as we held all responsibility for our four young campers. The girls assigned to our cabin were fun, lively, and competitive. It was sometimes challenging to balance our campers' unique personalities, but my co-counselor's energetic spirit encouraged the girls and helped sustain a positive atmosphere.

Being a counselor was exhausting, but sacred moments of joy and compassion filled my heart. Some nights, the girls would spend time chatting back and forth across their bunk beds, telling jokes or mentioning the latest celebrity gossip, the sound of laughter and happiness spilling out of our cabin windows into the peacefulness of the star-studded night.

---

16. Jon later became a mentor to an incredible little boy, too.

Mid-week during camp, there is always a special day des-ignated to celebrate "everybody's birthday."[17] The campers ex-perience an afternoon of jumping in bounce houses, stuffing plush animals full of fluff and accessorizing them Build-A-Bear style, and swimming at the pool decorated to the nines with Hawaii-themed décor. Volunteers blare on kazoos during din-ner, and many campers wear festive birthday party hats while consuming delicious pizza and inhaling sweet cupcakes. Right before bed, the campers return to their cabins to discover an assortment of gifts specially wrapped just for them!

That night, as our campers huddled around the carpet sur-rounded by the enormous bunk beds where we each slept, each girl's eyes sparkled as they excitedly unwrapped their presents. They took turns showing off their gifts, commenting about how amazing everything was, noticing if certain things matched their favorite color, and celebrating each present as a special blessing.

One exceptional quality all four of our girls expressed was their desire to help others. They were always eager to lend a helping hand, offering to share necessities like a hair scrunchie or sunscreen, and encouraging each other during challenging activities. I'll never forget when one of our campers extended this kindness to me. It was on Water Blast Day, and one of my friends (a fellow counselor) and her sister (my co-coun-selor) decided to sandwich me into a hug, their wet, shav-ing-creamed bodies smearing smooth, moist dollops of wa-tered-down cream all over me. I despise feeling grimy, and the textured irritation from the water and shaving cream dis-gusted me so much that my friend had to hold me for an extra minute because I was literally in tears from the messy

17. Children growing up in foster care don't always get to celebrate their birthdays, and some don't even know when their birthdays are, so RFKC always gives them a birthday party to remember!

sensation covering my body. After my friend's embrace, this camper noticed I was upset. She quickly grabbed a sponge full of water and began helping me wash off, her gentle voice telling me, "*It's okay, Miss Becca,*" as she carefully wiped off the cream saturating my arm. This simple act of kindness may have seemed insignificant, but the love I felt from her intentional care meant everything to me.

As tiresome as the week was, the satisfaction I felt watching each camper make positive memories, knowing that the power of Christ's love was sprinkled throughout every aspect of the week, outweighed my physical exhaustion. My heart beat with such love for these kids. I was grateful to be a part of their precious lives. The directors, counselors, and other volunteers sacrificed so much to create one impactful week for the campers, yet I doubt the campers realized how much their presence made a difference in our lives. No matter how exhausted I felt, I knew there was value in being a part of RFKC.

After a grueling week at camp, Jon and I reflected on the influence every volunteer made in the campers' lives.[18] We discussed the difficulty we had both felt being counselors yet recognized the life-changing effects one week had to transform our lives forever. Our hearts ached with compassion for the campers we met, and we believed that the seeds planted during camp were strong enough to make a difference.

As we talked about our camp experiences, we were confident that RFKC was an essential part of God's plan for our

---

18. Jon had his own challenging experiences that may have left him crying in the bathroom one night. Being a counselor is emotionally taxing.

lives and marriage. During the fall of 2017, Jon and I approached the camp directors (an incredible husband-and-wife duo) with a proposition we believed the Lord placed in our hearts: we wanted to become assistant camp directors.

After much prayer, a thorough explanation of the role, and a guarantee of our commitment to the position, the directors and church leadership approved our request to become assistant directors! We were so excited for all God had in store as we helped alleviate camp's planning responsibilities, a job that took ten months to prepare for one week of the year.

Our first year as assistant directors was filled with growing pains as the directors decided what responsibilities to give us while Jon and I figured out how to balance volunteering with our regular work hours. Walking alongside the directors during the week of camp in 2018 was beneficial for us to learn from their leadership and advice. When the next planning year started, Jon and I felt ready for more responsibility. We believed we were capable of leading and supporting the directors more. However, communication proved to be a challenge between the four of us. With our restricted schedules due to work and teaching, Jon and I needed advance notice to prepare for things, and sometimes we were confused by unclear communication. Although we loved the Royal Family KIDS ministry from the depths of our souls, volunteering in this assistant role was more challenging than we expected.

In the spring of 2019, we sought the Lord for wisdom. I journaled this simple desire to God and a verse He laid on my heart:

> "I believe with all my heart that you desire to use Jon and me in a ministry role to further impact your kingdom. Lead and guide us and reveal your will."

"Once these signs are fulfilled, do whatever your hand finds to do, for God is with you." (1 Samuel 10:7)

Camp 2019 was one to remember—not just because it was the last "real" camp before COVID hit. This was our second camp as assistant directors, and that year, we received more responsibility and reliance on our leadership. Numerous returning volunteers mentioned how relaxed and available the directors were that year, thanking Jon and me for our partnership with them and giving them a chance to experience camp to its fullest.

That summer, Jon and I were unexpectedly asked to consider becoming camp directors. Since my involvement with RFKC, only once had I thought about becoming an official director, a dream that I simply believed was just that—*a dream*. Now, that dream could become my reality! Ultimately, my soul cowered in fear at the request. I worried about the weight of responsibility and how Jon and I could balance such an important position when being assistants was already difficult. However, I remembered the promise found in 1 Samuel 10:7 and knew our passion for foster care was there for a reason. Jon's motivation for us to become directors bolstered my excitement for the leadership opportunity.

Before accepting the joint position, we were transparent with the missions pastor about our need for extra support due to our full-time work schedules and the demands of volunteering as directors.[19] With the pastor's promise to help us and hope embedded within our hearts, Jon and I were in anticipation of all God would do through us to serve children in foster care.

That November in 2019, I journaled this entry to the Lord:

---

19. At our church, every position with RFKC was volunteer, and the director role was a full-time commitment.

"I've felt so overwhelmed with gratitude recently. I've received countless compliments on my teaching efforts, and we've had many encouraging comments toward our leadership of RFKC. It's a very busy time in our lives, and I'm so thankful that our efforts are valued. I pray these encouragements continue in order to motivate us toward the goal ahead. Father, continue to use us and place us where we need to be. Utilize and equip us for each opportunity. Grow us so that we learn to live for you alone. Strengthen our marriage. Use us together for your glory."

Afterward, I felt God speak these words of comfort and affirmation, saying:

"I have called you for such a time as this to make a difference in the lives of those affected by foster care. I have anointed and equipped you to lead and have challenged you to grow. I am pleased by your obedience...and I am excited to see you learn and grow this season. I will never give you more than you can handle, for I have properly equipped you for what's at hand, you need only trust and rely on me and I will make it happen...Continue to serve me with all your heart, and I will be found."

Wow. What a beautiful responsibility God felt we were worthy to fulfill in becoming directors of RFKC. Our hearts were humbled in gratitude to the Lord for using us for something so much bigger than we could ever have imagined. Understanding that His purpose was being fulfilled by our obedience to serve felt empowering. We moved forward into the planning season for Camp 2020 with faith in the Lord's promised provision.

━◦━━ ━━◦━

Back in the spring of 2019, I randomly decided to browse through an old journal from high school, and I came across one particular entry from my post-graduation summer of 2010. When I read it, I was astonished that what I had journaled nine years earlier was currently coming true! The entry said:

> *"Right now my passion is not missions but children, **even orphans**, maybe even here in the USA, because I feel like I need to view my country as a mission field, not just go on mission trips."*

I could not believe it. I remembered telling the Lord I wanted to work with children after high school, but the *orphan* part of my desire had been omitted from my memory. When I wrote this journal entry, I had no idea what future God had in store for me. All I knew was that it involved children, and I was adamant to follow every step of the Lord's plan to accomplish His will in my life. At the time, I remember reading John 14:18, which says, "I will not leave you as orphans; I will come to you," and thinking about the orphans I had met during mission trip outreaches. I desired to care for orphans, but I didn't know how that would be possible in the States. I didn't know if working with orphans was actually a part of God's plan for my life, so I simply left my thoughts to the seclusion of my journal and continued my pursuit of God's will. When I became a teacher, I thought that was the extent of my life's calling, yet now I see that God had even more planned. By volunteering with (and then leading!) RFKC, I was literally living out my eighteen-year-old prayer-filled dreams.[20]

When I reflect on the reality of this journal entry and how it came to fruition in my life, I see the promise of Psalm 32:8 (NLT) as it declares, "The LORD says, 'I will guide you along the best pathway for your life. I will advise you and watch over you.'" That's exactly what God did for me. The Lord directed my steps, advised my choices, saw me through every obstacle, and campaigned my way to achieve these dreams. Through every doubt, testing roadblock, and even my fears of directing RFKC, God strategically brought my life full circle. My journal was evidence that I *had* walked in obedience to the Lord's will for my life, and He had brought me to my identity in a deeper way.

In Romans 8:28 (NLT), the Apostle Paul shares this truth: "And we know that God causes everything to work together for the good of those who love God and are called according to his purpose for them." God works everything out for those who love Him. This means when I do my best to live out the purpose He intends for my life through faith and obedience, He is faithful to cause good things to happen. This doesn't mean that my life will be filled with perfection and ease, but it does mean that the more I pursue a relationship with my Savior, the more blessings I will reap from His loving care. My responsibility is to place my hope in His promises and believe He will redeem every circumstance into triumph for His glory in my life!

---

20. Although many children in the foster care system are not true orphans (children who have lost their birth parents), they do experience similar tragedies from being raised in the fractured system.

Chapter Six

The Pandemic

*"Often when you think you're at
the end of something, you're at the
beginning of something else."*

FRED ROGERS

Friday, March 13, 2020. It was about 7:45 a.m. when our staff meeting ended, and I was walking back to my classroom to inform my teaching assistant that this would be our last day in school. As I delivered the news to her, my hands were shaking, my voice trembled, and my eyes pooled with heavy tears. Students began arriving at school, and my assistant insisted that I take a moment to breathe, assuring me she didn't mind taking charge of our morning routines.

I opened the door to the walk-in storage closet, the only place I could find complete seclusion, and crept inside. As I shut the door quietly behind me, my body slowly slumped to the floor. Desperately, I gasped for air, attempting to stifle my sobs of grief and heartbreak. Less than twenty-four hours before, my administration team held an impromptu staff meeting where our superintendent explained, "It's not *if* we close; it's *when*." He was preparing us all for the school's anticipated shutdown.

Official mandates were occurring across the nation in response to the newly discovered—and rapidly spreading—Coronavirus, causing schools and businesses everywhere to close immediately. We couldn't quite comprehend the magnitude of this unknown illness, its detrimental effects triggering community shutdowns nationwide in hopes of protecting the health of its citizens. I couldn't believe the virus was affecting my life; part of me thought the Midwest, perhaps the whole United States, would be able to steer clear of the mysterious sickness. Realizing that I was leaving my class during such an uncertain time was dreadful. This was undoubtedly the worst "Friday the Thirteenth" of my life.

Teachers had less than seven hours to create three weeks' worth of lesson plans and collect any necessary materials for at-home learning—all while simultaneously managing class-room routines, teaching lessons, and caring for our students. Luckily, my first-grade teaching partner, Stephanie, and I relied on our classroom assistants for help in the morning while we worked to prepare distance learning packets. The reality of closing school consumed my thoughts as I forced my body to function. We planned, prepped, gathered, and sorted every-thing before dismissal—our last day together. Before my students left, I hugged each one as I handed them their at-home learning packets, telling them I'd see them in just three weeks once the spread of the Coronavirus was under control.

Throughout the coming days, local mandates and national orders were authorized until all citizens were required to quar-antine at home.[1] On March 24, I journaled:

> *"We're seven school days into the school closures/distance learning due to COVID-19. We now have a stay-at-home order and will get a misdemeanor if we leave the house outside of the order restrictions."*

Six short days later, I wrote:

> *"I can't even explain the time we're experiencing during this pandemic of COVID-19. Social distancing guide-lines have been pushed back to April 30. It is highly un-likely that we'll go back to school to finish the year. My heart is so sad..."*

The following week, my school decided to continue dis-tance learning for the remainder of the school year. I was

---

1. Aside from front-line workers and employees deemed *essential*.

devastated beyond belief. I felt betrayed not finishing my first year in first grade with my explorers, saddened we wouldn't be returning to the classroom. No more morning greetings, no more classroom management distractions, no more planning interactive lessons, no end-of-year party to celebrate. My whole reason for teaching was to be with my students, and if I couldn't do that, was I even a teacher? I was frustrated having finally accomplished my career dreams, now having it seemingly ripped from my grasp. What was I supposed to do if my life's purpose was taken away from me? Teaching was a huge part of my identity. It fueled my soul with passion, determination, and ambition. How was I going to find value within myself without it? Despite my disappointment, I knew difficult decisions had to be made. The pandemic precautions were a necessary inconvenience for everyone around the country (and the world) as our lives halted in compliance with quarantine.

⊰━ ● ━ ● ━⊱

On April 6, 2020, I journaled the details of what was supposed to be our return to the classroom:

> *"Today should've been the day that we returned to school, but it's not. Today, we get to maintain social distancing (six feet away) and provide our [students'] parents with enough materials to finish the school year at home. I'm devastated that I will never teach these kiddos in my classroom again. I just spent seven hours of my 'spring break' weekend at school preparing materials. It is heartbreaking to be in the classroom, knowing my students are not*

returning. Though all of this is completely heartbreaking,
I am thankful to still be teaching. I am grateful that my
students are safe and cared for. This is just really hard..."

I'll never forget placing all my students' belongings and new distance learning packets along the edge of the elementary lobby wall, wearing disposable gloves as I touched each bag to prevent contamination, and maintaining social distance between my coworkers as we waited for families to arrive to collect their students' things. When each of my student's families pulled up to the curb of the elementary entrance, I carried their bundle of supplies outside and placed it on a desk to be retrieved. The fear surrounding the rapid spread of COVID-19 and its unknown transmission hung heavily in the air as we cautiously interacted together, teachers and families, careful to respect each other's boundaries, each of us grieving the loss of this school year.

It was truly agonizing to be back at school, spotting the calendar still displaying March 13. I recorded a short video to share with the families about the details of distance learning, and I included a special statement to say how much I missed my students. In the video, I reminded them of the last memory verse we learned together. It was Deuteronomy 31:8, which states, "The LORD himself goes before you and will be with you; he will never leave you nor forsake you. Do not be afraid; do not be discouraged." I encouraged my explorers that even though we were all feeling frustrated, afraid, and discouraged, God tells us He is always with us, and He will never leave us no matter what! It was humbling to realize that this verse was assigned to our Bible lesson the week before the pandemic "began," a time when we all needed assurance that God was in control and He still had a plan for *good* amidst the chaos.

During the abrupt transition to distance learning, minimal instruction was required by the elementary teachers at my school. Teachers were given the option to pre-record lessons and post them on their classroom Teams page to enhance learning and comprehension of important topics.[2] No live lessons or virtual Zoom meetings were scheduled unless a teacher arranged a session at their leisure. Otherwise, teachers simply created weekly lesson plans for families to complete with their students independently.

I missed the social aspect of my job immensely, and it was nearly impossible to maintain relationships with my students through distance learning. In May, I decided to host Saturday morning Zoom sessions with my class, which I cleverly titled *"Live! With Mrs. Kolenda."* During these live sessions, I planned discussion topics for each explorer to share, giving every student individualized screen time to talk, and I selected a special read-aloud story to share with the class. *Live! With Mrs. Kolenda* was such a special time to see many of my students, their sweet smiles and adorable banter cultivating joy in my heart. The grief I'd been carrying throughout the weeks of uncertainty and isolation diminished with each laugh we shared across the computer screen. The reality of the pandemic and the experiences that threw every routine into disarray were unthinkable, yet the simple joy of socializing over virtual meetings was irreplaceable.

---

2. Yes, we utilized Microsoft Teams for our distance learning platform. It's not the most elementary-friendly program, in case you were wondering.

On a particularly bleak and rainy evening that April, Jon and I were watching TV when a rush of anxiety startled me. Every breath felt like heaves of angst within my lungs, the rapid pace of concern hastening inside my chest. My heart felt like it was beating ninety miles a minute. I didn't know where the anxiety came from, but I knew my body needed immediate release from its strain. Suddenly, I leaped up from the couch and marched outside into the wet, dark night.

Jon followed me, confused, and repeatedly asked, "What's going on?" But I couldn't verbalize what was happening.[3] It felt like I was internally suffocating, something restricting me so hard I couldn't move. In hopes of relief, I spent about fifteen minutes pacing our backyard while light sprinkles of rain settled on my shoulders, the night air gently calming my heightened nerves. As my breath became steady and the whirlwind of fear inside my mind ceased, I calmly strolled back to the house feeling entirely exhausted.

At this moment, the stress of my circumstances caused me to panic. The fear surrounding COVID-19, the seclusion of quarantine, the loss of the school year, and the apprehension of the unknown future became too much for me to bear. Schedules, routines, to-do lists, and expectations have always provided stability in my life, but now those structures were gone from my day-to-day living. I tried to find security in being quarantined at home with Jon and did what I could to adapt to the changes, but the lack of control and constant fear were unsettling. It was difficult to cope while everything in life felt like it was being taken away. I had to wonder: *Where was God's purpose—where was my value—in all of this?*

---

3. Although I tried to communicate by shouting seemingly nonsense banter as I darted out the back door.

＋—■ ■—＋

Amid the pandemic, Jon and I had important decisions to make regarding RFKC. It was our first year as camp directors, and we knew that hosting camp in person that summer was going to be difficult, requiring accommodations due to COVID-19 mandates and restrictions. In early May 2020, I journaled:

> "No one can guarantee what the future holds in July. Our hearts ache because we know after this pandemic and isolation, these kids NEED to come to camp. But, we have to consider the health risks and safety of our staff and kids. If camp is able to happen, it won't look the same, so we have to take the right precautions…There's so many unknowns and this virus is serious, but our hearts just long for these kids to experience camp…Stay-at-home order in effect until May 15. State of emergency extended until May 28."

Two weeks later, I wrote this simple entry:

> "Well, all of the announcements have been made. Camp 2020 is not happening in the traditional sense. [The church] made the decision Tuesday night and our campground closed on Wednesday. Emails went out to our staff on Thursday, and we put together a completely new training for our staff on Saturday morning."

The official decision not to host camp made Jon and I feel whiplashed, all our previous planning efforts torn apart, every attempt to reconfigure our volunteer training into an online experience unhinged. We didn't know how the ministry was going to move forward amidst the pandemic. Even though we understood the safety concerns and mandates that influenced the cancelation of camp, the decision still grieved our hearts. Jon and I knew our campers would be missing a vital part of their summer, especially after months of social isolation, and we felt helpless not being able to support them during such a difficult time.

Not hosting camp as first-year directors was discouraging. Jon and I believed the Lord had called us to lead RFKC, but I didn't understand why God was making it impossible for us to achieve our calling. If He had planned for us to be directors, why weren't things working out perfectly? I didn't understand why doing the Lord's will was so complicated.

Despite our frustration and grievances, Jon and I were adamant about upholding the core values of Royal Family KIDS by striving to treat people royally, make moments matter, and *keep moving forward*, even amidst the hurdles of a worldwide pandemic! Our disappointment was not going to stop us from leading a new option to reach children in foster care.

We immediately began devising new plans for an impactful camp alternative. Jon and I attended several virtual meetings with RFKC headquarters and led numerous Zoom calls with our local leadership team. Ultimately, it was decided that our chapter would create a portable version of camp, brilliantly titled "Camp in a Box." This alternative provided a physical representation of the camp experience, including special mementos that each camper would have received during camp, like envelopes of encouraging "heart note" cards written by camp volunteers, a handmade quilt that a local church annually donates, a new Bible, and a photo album of camp memories. Other items representing specific events during camp were included, such as a summer craft and costume accessory for the activity center, and a birthday crown and present for Birthday Party Day. Additionally, a DVD of the daily Bible lessons and most popular songs was created by our volunteers so the campers could experience those entertaining elements of camp. "Camp in a Box" was truly a tangible example of the impactful moments RFKC creates to make a positive difference.

─────

In August, we scheduled a weekend for our volunteers to help package each box for the participating campers. Sign-ups were mandatory to regulate the number of people gathered, masks were required to prevent the spread of germs (whether COVID or otherwise), and stations were spread out to provide space for social distancing. Detailed packaging instructions were used to bundle every "Camp in a Box" item, and directions were posted to guide volunteers to each packing station.

Well over a dozen volunteers participated in preparing "Camp in a Box." Although our team was small compared to our normal camp roster, each volunteer was essential to the success of the camp alternative. Every person involved brought genuine care and enthusiastic faith to the packaging experience. As first-year directors, Jon and I were humbled by God's faithfulness in bringing our team together and making a difference for our campers. We may not have been at the campground, but our team was dedicated to doing whatever we could to reach out and be there for the children.

The following weekend, our leadership team made personal deliveries of "Camp in a Box." The delivery teams briefly stopped at each residence to open the camp alternative with the campers. One of the campers I had the pleasure of delivering to told me, "Tell everyone that the strong man's still alive." Although his sentiment was outrageously funny and such a "him" thing to say, the reality of the COVID-19 pandemic was evident in his comment: He wanted the Royal Family team to know that he was still *alive*, healthy, safe, and fine because for so many people, loved ones weren't okay and some were dying. As we finished going through his "Camp in a Box," we commented on each item, reminisced about past camp memories, and grieved the disappointment of not being at camp physically. But then, this camper made an impactful statement: "Well, God made a way."

His remark took me aback. Even though we weren't at camp, our team still put forth the effort to show our campers that we cared, and that made a positive impact. Somehow, God really *did* make a way.

Despite the restrictions and precautions of the COVID-19 pandemic, RFKC was able to create positive memories for the children we served. Jon and I were proud of our leadership efforts and grateful that our team still had the opportunity to be examples of Christ's love and make a difference in each camper's life. Although our passion and expertise had equipped us to lead, we knew it was the Lord who made it all possible.

This experience taught me that the value of God's purpose isn't meant to be in the *doing* of my calling but in the *trusting* of my faith. My constant efforts to achieve in life stemmed from my desire for stability. The more I did to manage my environment, the more secure I felt. Realizing that I not only needed to *do* God's will but also *trust* in His plan was an eye-opening lesson. When Camp 2020 was canceled, it felt like I had lost all control. I didn't know how to do my job as a director if camp wasn't happening. This was a huge opportunity for me to practice trusting the Lord and believe that He had an alternative plan. Every ounce of my control was gone, and I had to rest in the stability of my faith in Christ, which evidently led to the success of "Camp in a Box." Leading through the pandemic reiterated the reality that God may have designated Jon and me to be directors, but He was the one in ultimate control. Our responsibility was to trust in His sovereignty, and God would be faithful.

The end of summer meant one thing: a new school year! Although the pandemic was still occurring, communities were beginning to adjust to the "new normal" of post-quarantine life. My school's administration team and the school board deliberated whether current mandates and health protocols would allow for a return to in-person learning. Ultimately, they decided returning to the classroom was essential, and teachers were welcomed back into the building in mid-August to prep for the year ahead.

During the first week of school, I wrote two journal entries describing my feelings about being back in the classroom:

> *"Today is the first day of school! We haven't been in the building together for six months. I have so many nerves about today. I am so excited to be back at school!"*

"I feel so blessed, grateful, happy, content, satisfied, at peace, appreciative, thankful, excited, and fulfilled being back in the classroom."

After the way the last school year ended over distance learning, it felt so good to be in person with my new batch of first-grade explorers! I leaped back into the fulfillment of my career joyfully. I was eager to experience all the personal connections I had missed during quarantine and take full advantage of my time in person with my students.

However, being together in the classroom wasn't the same as it had been before the pandemic. Routines had to be adapted to follow safety measures to keep the spread of COVID at bay. Students' desks were required to be at least three feet apart, no carpet time was allowed, and students could remove their masks only when sitting alone at their desks. Hand sanitizer was used constantly, and shared materials were kept at a minimum (and sanitized profusely). On a good day, it's difficult to teach a six-year-old to wash their hands after going to the bathroom or not to lick their fingers, so these strict rules were exhausting to implement (especially on top of teaching). Teachers returned to the classroom in hopes that it would feel normal, but it was a challenge acclimating to how these new protocols influenced the socializing, learning, instructing, and sanitizing of our daily routines.

Despite the demands of post-COVID regulations, I felt fortunate to be in person with my students. Many schools around the nation were teaching entirely virtually that school year or were implementing a "hybrid" version of online and in-person instruction. Every day, I savored the opportunity to see my students. I loved hearing the sound of their laughter, listening to their stories, and watching their eyes light up as they learned. It was far from pleasant wearing a mask all day while I taught, giving endless reminders about social distancing, mask-wearing, and hand sanitizing to fifteen six- and seven-year-olds, yet I was beyond grateful to simply *be* with my students.

Due to the potential spread of COVID-19, it was important for schools and businesses to have health protocols in place to mitigate the illness. If in-person instruction was deemed impossible because of health concerns, we would have to resort to distance learning again. At my school, distance learning was going to be structured differently than last year, requiring teachers to instruct virtual lessons over a Teams video call every weekday. Teachers attended numerous meetings and training sessions to learn more about online instruction and virtual teaching techniques, which added to the pressure of teaching during the pandemic.

Inevitably, my school did have to revert to distance learning during the school year. When the first virtual week of school occurred after Thanksgiving break that November, I wrote these entries about my experience:

> *"I got to go back to school today, but not in person with my students, and that's making me very upset."*

> *"Well, today is our first virtual instruction online. I'm excited to see my kiddos, but dreading any technical issues. This is very mentally taxing and emotionally draining..."*

"Distance Learning went well yesterday, although it makes me ten times more exhausted. Between watching two monitors, being animated and 'on' the entire time, having patience calling on students, or with tech issues... Simply exhausting!"

Teaching virtually was an experience unlike any other.

Just imagine being logged into a Teams meeting with fifteen young children. While you're leading a presentation about verbs, you notice a half-naked toddler on someone's computer screen. You ignore the sight as the child runs off-camera and proceed to ask for a volunteer to share their knowledge about verbs. You select someone to answer and wait several seconds as they unmute their mic, but the audio delay from their connection causes confusion and you begin to talk over their lagged video.

The presentation continues as you attempt to re-engage the group by sharing an example of verbs using the "share screen" feature, which unexpectedly freezes on everyone's computer screens. As you try to reconnect your device, you notice that two people have dropped off the meeting and need your assistance getting back in. Once they return, you try to recompose yourself and remember where you left off, simultaneously checking all fifteen cameras to make sure everyone is there and ready to participate.

Then, you notice one screen showing someone's forehead while another screen displays an entirely empty bedroom waiting for your engaging presentation to continue. This makes you very frustrated, but you take a breath and resume the verb presentation you spent time creating outside of your contracted hours. You glance at the clock and realize this chaotic experience took twenty minutes of the thirty minutes you al-lotted for the entire presentation.

This dramatic (yet realistic) description is what it was like teaching first grade online every day. Entirely exhausting.

After that shutdown, my school remained in-person for most of the school year. Minimal classrooms required periodic quarantine, and distance learning was only necessary school-wide twice more.[4] It was scary to put yourself and your students' health at risk against a seemingly invisible illness. The severity of the disease was constantly broadcasted, restrictions still mandat-ed nationwide, and people were beginning to develop differing opinions about the entire purpose of the pandemic. All I want-ed was to guarantee the health and safety of my students and mitigate our chances of possible quarantine. Being in person with my class where I could productively teach, advocate for my students' needs, and build a class community was important to me. Our time together was truly invaluable.

This group of students was genuinely heaven-sent during this abnormally hectic school year. As a teacher, there are unique years when it seems that all your students get along and build supportive relationships with each other, and the entire class respectfully obeys (almost) every instruction. Educators often refer to these unusual groups of students as a "unicorn class." This class was full of magical unicorns. And to my delight, they seemed to like me, which aided the positivity of our learning environment (and boosted my self-esteem).

---

4. Some cases of COVID-19 were classroom or grade-level specific and did not spread school-wide.

One day, I planned a craftivity for the students to create a "sentence buddy" since we were learning about the characteristics of a complete sentence.[5] The activity greatly interested the group, and various students began exclaiming:

"You're the best teacher!"

"Yeah, you're the best teacher ever!"

"Yeah, we love you!"

"We never wanna leave you!"

"Yeah, we want you to be our teacher forever!"

I remember simply laughing in that moment, perplexed by their devotion yet thankful for their love toward me as their teacher. Hearing such adoring comments from my students filled my teacher's heart to the brim with joy. Expressions of gratitude, love, and appreciation constantly exuded from my explorers that year. Once during lunchtime, one of my students prayed, "Thank you for making us in first grade to be with the best teacher, Mrs. Kolenda." And on a particularly low-key, "busywork" day I scheduled to finish student assessments, an explorer exclaimed, "Today was so easy! Thank you so much!"

Being back in the classroom was refreshing, especially feeling so valued by my students. Their endearment toward me made every obstacle that year worth it. I was incredibly grateful that the Lord had given me such a redemptive class after the trauma from the last school year. Each year has something special to appreciate about its group of students or something that happens to positively impact the class community, but that year was epic. It was my unicorn class.

---

5. An activity turned into a craft. After writing a complete sentence (the activity), the students added labels to the sentence strip to create a "buddy" figure (the craft).

As I acclimated to my school routine, planning for next summer's camp began. Balancing career and ministry responsibilities during the pandemic was challenging, to say the least. Although I had managed these same expectations most of last year, the weight of responsibility changed. Previous time-management strategies, planning routines, and productivity habits that had sustained my career-ministry schedule weren't working. I was trying to accomplish tasks at a normal pace, but adjusting back to regular life during the pandemic was anything but *normal*. Plus, the mantle's lasting impact crushed my self-esteem as I expected idealized efforts from myself. My emotional and mental stamina were exhausted from the stress of it all, and the year was just beginning! In the fall of 2020, I journaled my struggles to the Lord, saying:

"I got overwhelmed last night after doing some RFKC work. I had a bit of an anxiety attack. I hate that that happens. I just get stressed and consumed with all the 'to-dos' to run RFKC well, especially when Jon isn't available to help me."

Finding time to complete tasks for camp preparations was difficult because my teaching hours weren't flexible, and I often had additional projects to complete outside of my contracted eight-hour day. Plus, Jon worked more than ten hours a day, along with taking college courses toward his MBA. Most of our weekday evenings consisted of a forty-five-minute dinner together, then I worked on RFKC tasks for about three hours before heading to bed, and Jon would complete his homework assignments until ten p.m. (on a good night) or two a.m. (on a typical night). Our nonexistent "weekends" were a mix of completing camp to-dos, school assignments, or household chores. Jon either helped with camp preparations or spent his time working on his MBA projects and attending group meetings. This constant pace of life was physically exhausting, and the mental stress was unbearable.

During that time, I came across an inspiring scripture that uplifted my spirits and encouraged my soul. I journaled the verse along with my sentiments:

"'...I am weary, God, but I can prevail.' (Proverbs 30:1)

"I love that word 'prevail.' Even when I'm weary of doing good or weary of my responsibilities, I CAN still prevail. God is with me! So much can be changed just by a better outlook and a positive attitude. Lord, in my moments of weariness, help me to stay the course! **PREVAIL**— *I won't just 'make it' or 'get by.' I will be victorious and prevail over the overwhelming circumstance!"*

How uplifting is that?! At such a pivotal time of responsibility in my life, I felt the Lord was preparing me to understand that by doing His will, I would *prevail*. I might experience momentary stress, but God would give me the endurance to continue moving forward into a victorious future. However, even though I was inspired to cling to the truth of this scripture, I was too overwhelmed by anxiety to believe in its power. As encouraging as this revelation was to my weary soul, I soon forgot its significance and turned my attention back to the stress of my reality.

The long hours of school responsibilities and RFKC tasks felt like weeks, the fast-paced days of constant to-dos felt like years, and the drawn-out months of planning and preparing felt like an eternity to my downcast and overworked self. Jon and I were the first camp directors of our local chapter where both spouses had full-time careers, and the volunteer expectations of the director role were not conducive to regular work schedules. The way that our RFKC chapter was structured, the directors oversaw every aspect of running camp and were in charge of many of those responsibilities, like staff recruitment, planning and running staff training, creating the camp schedule, managing the overall budget, and working with the state of Michigan and local campground for our annual licensing renewal, just to name a few. This year, our chapter didn't have a full-time admin or child placement coordinator, which meant our list of duties was even more extensive.

At the end of 2020, I wrote this journal entry:

"I had a complete breakdown last night. The last two days, I've experienced horrible anxiety...I struggle doing two large jobs at once, and Jon is so busy with school and GM. We desperately need more reliable support! Go before us, Lord. We want to do your will, but are feeling so discouraged, overwhelmed, frustrated, and burnt out. I'm tired of struggling like this. I want to be able to focus on teaching and contribute to a ministry without breaking down and feeling miserable...Jesus, you need to move in our circumstance..."

In His graciousness, God met me in my misery and spoke these words of wisdom to my heart:

"I've equipped you for such a time as this. I will be with you and walk with you through the fire. My hand of anointing will be on you. Seek me and you will find me. Trust me, and I will lead and guide you. Great things are in store for you! I will bless you and protect you. I have called you for a purpose. Continue to seek me and do my will. Love me with your whole heart."

I felt emotionally depleted and physically drained directing RFKC and teaching simultaneously. My time was entirely divided by demanding responsibilities with no breaks for reprieve. I believed that the Lord had destined me for this purpose and that He would be with me through every challenge, but I doubted the blessing of it all. I didn't understand why, if God had *"equipped me for such a time as this,"* I wasn't feeling more confident. My identity and value were tied to the way my passions and purpose made me feel, so why wasn't doing the Lord's will bringing me a sense of satisfaction and worth? I heard God's wisdom when He answered me in my distress, but I didn't want an ambiguous solution to my problems. I needed physical relief or else I was going to collapse under the pressure.

Our church provided the opportunity for us to be mentored by previous camp directors. Jon and I learned a great deal from their advice and appreciated their support, but we still needed help alleviating the responsibilities of our long to-do list. We decided that delegation was the solution to our problem. Even though we had a supportive leadership team, we were protective of their contributions, not wanting to cause burnout in their lives or volunteer commitments. Jon and I determined that recruitment was our only option to find someone willing to partner with us and help remove some of the planning load.

However, we quickly learned that drafting anyone into a time-consuming volunteer position is nearly impossible. People are generally too busy with life, careers, or family to give time toward such a demanding commitment, or sometimes people simply value their free time and don't want to be overburdened by responsibility, prioritizing a life-work balance. Although we understood people's decisions not to volunteer, it frustrated us (me especially) that more people weren't willing to help. We did gain some support from a few people and recruited a temporary child placement coordinator, but it wasn't enough to balance the stress of directing.

In addition to our overbearing list of duties, Jon and I were tasked with researching COVID-19 health protocols required to ensure our compliance with RFKC's accreditation. These guidelines would influence the modifications necessary to reconfigure camp's social structure and guarantee a safe (and legal) experience. I was distraught by the added encumbrance of research to my already overwhelming to-do list.

In February 2021, I journaled my frustration to the Lord:

"This season of life is ten times harder amidst the pandemic. It's really wearing me down…I am overwhelmed with beginning research to adapt camp plans…I don't see an end in sight, and that's really hard…The stress is just so overwhelming…Continue to help us, Lord."

Amidst my anguish, God reminded me of these promises:

"My Word says I will sustain you (Isaiah 46:4).

My Word says I will supply all of your needs (Philippians 4:19).

My Word says you can do all things through Christ (Philippians 4:13)."

Oh, how I wish I had accepted the Lord's encouragement, that I had chosen to find comfort in the truth of these verses. Yet, no matter how much God tried to uplift my distraught spirit, positive words brought no consolation to the turmoil overtaking my emotional stamina. I felt discouraged by my inability to endure this inspiring yet overwhelming purpose of impact. I didn't feel the Lord's strength, and I doubted how I was going to keep moving forward. The weight of responsibility was too much for me to bear.

In my despair, it was difficult to believe Jesus' words when He told His disciples, "…And be sure of this: I am with you always, even to the end of the age." (Matthew 28:20 NLT). Believing that God was with me, that He would always be with me, seemed impossible. I thought: *If God saw the extent of my suffering, why wasn't He stopping it?* Yet, even in my confusion, a small part of me knew it was true. God was with me, I just didn't grasp how close He actually was.

Even when we don't realize it, God is always with us—in dark, stormy nights and bright, pleasant days, in disparaging grief and elating happiness, in deplorable heartache and victorious triumphs. God promises never to leave us. Difficult circumstances are a part of our sin-fallen world, but there is hope in knowing that we are held carefully in the palm of the Lord's love and protection. King David explains this concept best:

"The Lord is my shepherd, I lack nothing. He makes me lie down in green pastures, he leads me beside quiet waters, he refreshes my soul. He guides me along the right paths for his name's sake. Even though I walk through the darkest valley, I will fear no evil, for you are with me; your rod and your staff, they comfort me... Surely your goodness and love will follow me all the days of my life..." (Psalm 23:1-4, 6)

When I was overwhelmed by responsibilities, I didn't know how to trust God to relieve my burdens. I didn't have the stamina to believe in a miraculous solution. All I could do was keep moving forward, carrying my anxiety and stress along with me. But in God's mercy, He stayed with me. It was far from an easy situation to walk through, but it was an opportunity for the Lord to show His grace, compassion, and sovereignty in my life. God was there in my struggle—sustaining me, leading me, equipping me—I just didn't believe it.

Chapter Seven

The Breaking Point

"God has ways to help us that we dream not of."

CHARLES SPURGEON

How did I end up here? After a long day of teaching, I pulled into the driveway of our home and stared at the front door. It was *open.* Instantly, panic gripped my heart and fear constricted my lungs. *Why was the front door wide open?*

Through heaves of terrified sobs, I called Jon to confirm if I should call 911. He was states away on a business trip in Tennessee, and I was all alone. After momentarily consoling myself, I dialed 911 and waited for the police to arrive. My heart pounded like a bass drum, my brain incapacitated by the emotional burdens of life, my consciousness unable to comprehend the reality of the open door in front of me. How did this happen?

Minutes later, two police officers arrived, parked behind my Buick Encore, and walked toward the front porch to begin their investigation. They searched the house, yelling "police" as they turned corners and entered different rooms, their fire-arms propped and ready to fire just like in the TV shows. I watched the glow of their flashlights illuminate throughout my home, bouncing off the windows, spotlighting whatever disturbances were to be discovered. It was a gut-wrenching, heart-dropping-into-your-stomach scene.

Finally, the officers finished their search and completed a walk-through of the house with me. It was determined that no break-in had occurred and that the house was safe. I reflected on the night before and remembered I had retrieved an Amazon package from the front porch and must have forgotten to lock the door. It had been an abnormally gusty day, so the high winds likely pushed it open.

Even though I knew my home was safe, I was afraid. My physical reality may have been secure, but my mental and emotional state were unsettled. The weight of stress, depression, and anxiety were shattering my stamina, and I couldn't manage any more instability. I felt myself buckling under the pressure of teaching, directing, living, and breathing. My responsibilities were becoming too much for me to handle. I was afraid of falling apart.

◦━━ ━━◦

Throughout the nine months of simultaneously directing Royal Family KIDS Camp and teaching during the pandemic, I experienced frequent breakdowns. The constant pace of life and the overbearing pressure of responsibility left me mentally, physically, and emotionally drained. During that time, I journaled about the persistent pressure of anxiety:

"I had a lot of heavy anxiety last night. Even though I know that I'm okay and that you always meet our needs, I don't know how to control this physical feeling of anxiousness. I don't know how to give it to you and be at peace because it's such a physical feeling."

"I experienced so much anxiety last night, more than I have in a while…I didn't sleep restfully, it's like a void full of anxiety and stress…I'm just feeling like a lot is on my shoulders…I don't enjoy being put under pressure. I don't know how to manage this anxiety. I'm literally sick to my stomach."

The physical feeling of stress was impossible to escape. No matter how much I prayed, how many deep breathing exercises I did, or how many positive affirmations I read, I remained trapped in a dark pit of anxiety.

In the spring of 2021, I had an overwhelming panic attack. I had just gotten home from a full day of teaching and was drowning in COVID-19 health research. I was downloading articles and policy guidelines, attempting to decipher which protocols were required by different authorities involved with state licensing for residential camps. Interpreting all the intricacies of the COVID-19 mandates felt impossible, and my perfectionist expectations made the task even more difficult.

To top it off, Jon wasn't going to make it home for dinner that night, which meant that when he was finished with work, we wouldn't get to spend any time together because he would need to finish his school assignments. This fact was enough to turn my universe topsy-turvy. The realization that any security, peace, or relief I desperately craved was unable to happen suppressed my every breath. Throughout our years together, Jon had become my safe place, a safety net for me to find comfort, love, and protection within. He is the one person I can rely on for much-needed co-regulation. Not having access to my husband's support during that stressful moment only exacerbated my breakdown.

Later that night, I journaled these details about this moment of panic:

> "I had a COMPLETE breakdown tonight...I was screaming, crying, smacking things, sitting on the ground. 'I can't do this.' 'I don't want to do this.' 'Why do I have to do this?' I'm upset with God that He wants me to go through this. It is too much for me."

Something inside me entirely erupted, exploding up from my gut into vicious tears and piercing screams. This was the most intense panic attack I had ever experienced. In my agitation, I began pacing the kitchen, walking circles around the island as I cried, shouting in frustration at God for making me go through this. Abruptly, I slumped to the floor, smacking my hands against the hardwood as tears began pooling into delicate puddles on the ground around me, the salty drops of despair falling from my weary eyes and rushing down my cheeks. Crouched in the fetal position, I began rocking back and forth with my arms crossed against my stomach, hoping to physically prevent myself from falling apart.

I cried until my tear ducts became dry, my throat parched, my lungs exhausted from the stressful struggle. At that moment, it felt like the essence of my being had been suffocated, the life entirely eradicated from my person. I had absolutely no motivation left to keep going. Confusion consumed my thoughts—*Why was God allowing this to happen to me?* If all this responsibility was a part of His master plan for my life's purpose, why wasn't He working out these issues for my benefit? Where was God's compassion and mercy amidst my anxiety? My expectation for perfection clouded my belief in the Lord's saving grace. I knew that I needed God's help to execute my calling as both a director and teacher, and I was beyond frustrated that He didn't seem to understand that.[1]

In 1 Peter 5:10 (NLT), Peter inspires the church elders with the following message: "…So after you have suffered a little while, he will restore, support, and strengthen you, and he will place you on a firm foundation."

The truth of this scripture is clear: When we experience suffering, God will be faithful to redeem our troubles. These panic attacks felt like internal suffering, and I desperately needed the Lord's promised restoration. The slightest nudge of anxiety made me feel the mantle's pressure of excellence all over again—feelings of disappointment, regret, and confusion

---

1. The lesson of "doing vs. trusting" took a while for me to learn.

taking over my mind. All I wanted was to obey the Lord's will and have things work out—was that too much to ask? I was convinced that unless God removed the stress and pressure from my life, I might not even survive, let alone be successful in my life's calling.

Though I was tormented with anxiety, the Lord was directing every detail to fall into place throughout the ten months of camp preparations. My human strength was failing me, but God's strength was supernaturally influencing everything to work for *good* and make Camp 2021 happen to the success of His undeniable faithfulness.

During the last few months of camp planning, several important details needed miraculous intervention. One issue was our staff roster. Due to the COVID-19 pandemic, social-distancing mandates required strict occupancy restrictions, which meant that our staff size and camper ratio would need to be cut in half. With a smaller camp size, Jon and I hoped this adjustment would be to our advantage, providing just the right number of counselors to pair with each camper and an efficient amount of support staff to fill other important roles. By God's grace, we recruited just the right number of volunteers needed, and enough counselors to partner with every child who applied to attend Camp 2021! It was truly amazing to see the Lord answer our staffing prayers.

Another need that had to be resolved involved the nightly drama performances during camp's chapel time. Due to COVID-19 precautions, we decided to pre-record the drama and show each skit digitally. To make this happen, we first needed a drama coordinator to lead this new adaptation. Back in 2018, our RFKC chapter had this same vacancy, and I suggested my mom fill the position. Mom had extensive theater experience throughout her childhood, and she led my youth group drama team at our church for several years. I knew she would love to be involved with camp. The only drawback was that she didn't live in Michigan. Be that as it may, the previous directors agreed to welcome my mom to Camp 2018, and she traveled more than four round trips (over 2,440 total miles) to lead the drama team that year!

This year, in a moment of déjà vu, Jon and I asked my mom to join Camp 2021. She had been supportive of our leadership from the beginning, and after her experience at camp in 2018, Mom was eager to help us in any way she could. With an enthusiastic "Yes!", she agreed to be the drama coordinator again.

Now that we had a drama coordinator, plans needed to be finalized to record the drama skits. A few months earlier, Jon and I received an email from a married couple who expressed interest in being involved with camp, but they could not commit the time to volunteer. As we reread their email, we noticed that their signature included their personal contact information for their professional videography business. I immediately emailed the couple back and asked if they'd be able to help us record the drama, and they graciously volunteered their services. My mom worked closely with the couple to schedule a recording date and finalized specific details for the video edits. The opportunity to have a professional videography company film each skit went above and beyond what we had desired. The drama is an entertaining part of chapel, but it also exemplifies biblical lessons for the campers to learn more about God's Word. This answered prayer was an example of

God's careful consideration to work out each minuscule detail for the betterment of camp's success, all to His glory.

Amidst all the stress, God truly was working everything for *good*. I journaled my gratitude to the Lord, telling Him:

> *"Lord, thank you for your faithfulness. Even though the responsibility of leading RFKC is unbearable, you continue to help every important detail fall into place... We are at our wits' end, but we know you'll carry us through."*

Despite the Lord's provision, I continued to battle anxiety and weariness. I could see God guiding every decision and plan for a successful camp experience, but the overwhelming feelings of exhaustion and pressure remained. That summer, I wrote this simple entry:

> *"Life is so constant. I get stressed just breathing."*

Even without the responsibility of teaching during the summer, I still felt like I was drowning under the weight of leadership. I didn't understand how God's plan for my life, something filled with so much *good* as volunteering with RFKC, was causing me such pain. The absence of relief made me question my life's identity. I was supposed to find value and worth in my life's calling, not despair and distress. Yet, all I could do was continue to walk in obedience to the Lord's will. If God genuinely wanted Jon and me to become directors, then I had to trust (even if my faith was smaller than a mustard seed like in Matthew 17:20) that He would be faithful to honor our sacrifices and help us through.

Finally, Camp 2021 arrived, the week I thought would never come! After experiencing the upheaval of Camp 2020 plans last summer, being at the campground as an official director was surreal. Tangibly seeing the fulfillment of all our planning efforts to make camp happen amid the pandemic was unbelievable. My breath was truly taken away by God's graciousness in making camp an extraordinary reality.

Before the campers arrived for the week, our team traveled to the campground to set up. We loaded a large box truck with items from an off-site storage facility full of games, bedding, shelves, sports equipment, tables, and so much more. Our volunteers spent all day Saturday unloading everything, setting up each area around the campground—activity center, woodworking, fishing, chapel, and a glorious store filled with numerous donations of clothes, toys, gadgets, and jewelry called "The Sunshine Shop."

That Saturday morning, as Jon and I pulled into the campground ahead of our volunteers' arrival, one of the volunteers had arrived early and went to the staff lodge to unpack his personal belongings. Within minutes, the volunteer returned and told us that a campground employee notified him that the staff lodge had been condemned and our volunteers were not permitted to stay there. *Are you kidding me?* The campers arrived in just two days, and the support volunteers had already been assigned to stay in the lodge for the entire week.

After speaking with the campground manager about the issue, there was no other alternative than to reconfigure previously planned (and socially distanced) sleeping arrangements.

Luckily, because of the accommodations we made to have a smaller staff roster and camper ratio, there was space to spare in the cabins.[2] For the next hour or so, I worked with our mentoring director to re-adjust the lodging assignments, still accounting for necessary social distancing regulations. When the adjustments were finalized, I stood back and stared at the reconfigured list, astounded by God's faithfulness. It was clear that the Lord already knew this issue would happen, and He worked it out seamlessly.

At 7 a.m. on Monday, the registration team began directing each camper and their foster parent through the required stations—confirming their guardians' contact information, providing medication to our licensed nurse, dropping off their luggage, and getting their camp t-shirt and nametag.[3] While the registration process was well underway, Jon realized that the bus hadn't yet arrived.[4] We needed to begin loading the campers' belongings before it was time to board the bus for our trip to the campground. Jon repeatedly called the bus company, but their dispatch office didn't open for another hour. It was already thirty minutes past the bus's arrival time, and I was stressed. Finally, Jon got ahold of dispatch, and we learned that the assigned driver for our pick-up didn't show up for work that morning. The company immediately called an off-duty employee to drive us to camp as soon as possible.

As Jon and I managed that hiccup, we had to remind ourselves that God was in control of every circumstance,

2. The cabins were normally designated for counselor and camper pairings.
3. Foster parents, adoptive parents, social workers, or guardians typically drop off the campers.
4. Both registration and pick-up are done at the church instead of at the campground.

especially when we learned that a particular camper was hesitant to complete the registration process. He was a returning camper, but this was his first time coming to camp without his older siblings, and he seemed nervous to attend without them. Different volunteers tried to encourage him and alleviate his concerns, but no one could convince him to stay.

The camper's adoptive mom mentioned an errand she needed to run, and she urged her son to finish registration so he could enjoy a fun week at camp. One of our lead volunteers suggested that the camper could run the errand with his family, and she would meet his mom later to bring him to camp. This solution satisfied the camper, and his mother gratefully agreed.

Later that afternoon, the camper arrived at camp with no sign of reluctance. He joined right in with the other campers at the playground, making conversation and joining in their games. Throughout the week, the camper always wore a smile as he played at activity center, fished at the pond, splashed in the pool, or ate second helpings at dinner. Everything he did at camp seemed to fill his bucket to the brim with happiness.

When I reflect on the stress of that Monday morning, I now see God's plan so clearly. I may have experienced anxiety when the bus was two hours late, but that lag time was necessary for this camper. If the bus had been on time, the registration process would've moved faster, putting even more pressure on his decision. And maybe his mom wouldn't have mentioned her errand, and the camper wouldn't have felt comfortable attending camp at all. Even though my plans fell through, God's plan succeeded. The Lord used the downtime of the late bus to make a way for this camper to come to camp and have the best time of his life.

Camp 2021 was truly the most humbling week of my life. Experiencing the unity between our team and watching each volunteer step into their designated role was inspiring. Seeing the campers' eyes light up throughout each day, knowing that Christ's love was integrated into everything the campers did, brought joy to my heart. Campers will often ask our volunteers how much they're paid to spend the week at camp, and each time, the camper is astonished that the volunteers *pay* to attend camp. Our staff give their time, money, and energy to serve these deserving kids, and the positive difference that camp makes is worth every sacrifice.

Unless you've been to camp and have felt the passion that emanates throughout the atmosphere, it's impossible to describe what being a part of Royal Family KIDS is like. That year, it was even more astounding to me that the ten months of planning Jon and I invested alongside our leadership team amounted to this inspiring week of life-changing moments— both for us, our volunteers, and our campers. Many of our staff praised the success of our leadership during Camp 2021 and said it was "the best week of camp ever." Jon and I felt undeserving of such gratitude, acknowledging that every success during the week was a testament to God's unmerited goodness and abundant faithfulness.

As Camp 2021 came to a close, the truth of Psalm 128:1-2 resonated in my heart: "Blessed are all who fear the Lord, who walk in obedience to him. You will eat the fruit of your labor; blessings and prosperity will be yours." Despite all the stress, despair, and frustration I felt while planning camp, my biggest priority was to follow God's plan. Jon and I believed in RFKC, and we had seen the positive impact it made in people's lives, especially for the children we served. We believed in the ministry's mission to make a difference. Even when the responsibilities of directing tested our faith and my anxiety threshold, we chose to lead with utmost devotion to the Lord's call on our lives. He was faithful to bring blessing and prosperity from our obedience. The reality of camp's success put into perspective that our purpose in being directors wasn't in the act of directing but in our willingness to facilitate God's plan for the ministry. Our physical efforts may have influenced parts of the planning process, but it was God's influence that made the impact.

The week after camp, I briefly journaled my gratitude to the Lord:

"Thank you, Lord, for being faithful. The week of camp was truly special. I hadn't been that calm and relaxed in months…"

It was bizarre how calm my spirit felt being at camp, all the tension from the stress of planning evaporating in the tranquility of the week. It was as if I had been wearing an ornate cape designed with oppression and despair, and once I arrived at camp—with every preparation and plan in place—I unfastened the cape's clasp and the negativity woven onto it fell from my weary shoulders. Experiencing inner peace felt surreal after so many months of overbearing anxiety.

However, as I acclimated to regular life after camp, I began wrestling with a terrible question: *Why did I feel like I had been abused?*

Despite the peace I had while at camp, I felt used and emotionally mistreated. How did this make any sense? I had been safe at camp, and I knew that every person under our leadership was supportive and loving. Serving RFKC was a selfless, God-ordained *good* thing to do, so what made me feel this way? It was as if I had returned to my childhood, sitting on the couch while my parents fought, watching their dispute flair up as I internally struggled to find security. The environment of directing RFKC was nothing like my upbringing, yet I was having identical feelings of trauma.

As I processed these feelings with Jon one night, he nonchalantly said, "Maybe it's because of the anxiety you experienced growing up." I was dumbfounded by his statement; I had anxiety as a child? I remember feeling pressure throughout my childhood—pressure from the mantle to be perfect, please others, and protect my brothers—but I never identified the internal stress as *anxiety*...not until now, twenty-nine years later.

It was difficult to process that I had grown up with anxiety. I couldn't believe that my little, innocent self had experienced such overbearing stress, nor the fact that I continued to suffer from its pressure. I reflected on the panic attacks that defined certain moments of my life, realizing their origin came from the trauma of my childhood. Anxiety has followed me throughout my entire life, flowing through my veins like the necessity of oxygen. It's something I never knew existed let alone was attached to my mental well-being. As an adult, I learned the concept of anxiety as being an emotional reaction to stress, but until this epiphany, I never realized the potential of my chronic problem. It appeared that my mind had developed a coping strategy to view stress as something dangerous, causing me panic, misery, and apprehension when put under pressure. However, when I had a break from expectations and responsibilities, my mind thought I was safe, allowing me to feel relaxed and at peace. Being at camp gave me a break from the constant to-dos and planning responsibilities, causing my spirit to finally rest and breathe. But when I returned home, back to the normal pace of plans and duties, I felt stressed again. The pressure of directing triggered a learned stress response that my mental safety had been taken advantage of, and I subconsciously related the feeling to my experiences growing up.

I was grateful to understand the reason for my current feelings, but I was distraught by the genesis of it all. Why did my past hurt have to intrude upon my healed future? I was frustrated by the damage done during my childhood, discouraged that it was still impacting me as an adult. I thought that following the Lord's will and accepting His purpose for my life would rectify the pain of my past. Why was I *still* hurt and broken? I was doing everything I could to restore my future. Would I ever find true healing from my past trauma?

After experiencing this challenging season, I discovered the blessing of hindsight. It is an opportunity to reflect on a moment in time that influenced where you've arrived in the present day. Processing the effects of this life chapter—which I lovingly refer to as the era of *trials and tribulations* for its emotional hardship and overbearing responsibilities—has been the hardest for me to gain clarity. Yet somehow, I can see God's divine intervention during those difficult years.

I don't know if I'll ever understand why I had to experience such soul-crushing anxiety nor why—despite my best efforts to obey God and seek deliverance—my faith was utterly depleted. Perhaps it was the accumulation of anxiety and trauma that I never fully processed. Whatever the reason, I do know that if those years had gone differently, I wouldn't have appreciated my healing journey to the extent that I do now.

The suffering and confusion caused by those years of overwhelming responsibility reopened a deep wound only Jesus could heal. As I continued to walk in (imperfect) obedience to His will, God was gracious to bring the healing my heart desperately needed. I do not believe that the Lord destined this season to bring me to ruin. He simply desired my faithfulness toward His sovereignty despite the chaos of my circumstances.

One lesson I've learned through hindsight is that although I heard God's voice—He did answer my outcries of desperation—I didn't *listen*. To *listen* to someone means paying attention to what they are saying, giving thought and consideration to what is being expressed. However, to simply *hear* someone speak, you are perceiving the sound, and you know that they're talking, but you're not processing meaning from the noise.

Hearing is effortless; listening is intentional.

In the spring of 2019, while we were debating whether to continue being assistant directors of RFKC, the Lord spoke this truth to my heart:

> *"You're right where I need you to be. Don't falter to the right or left. Keep your eyes fixed on me. Truly I tell you, I am doing a work and you will make a difference. Just trust me. This season will not last forever. I have created you for bigger things. Let this time mold you and grow you. Just do what you can. I will equip you for what's to come. 'Be patient in affliction, faithful in prayer' (Romans 12:12). 'See, I am doing a new thing! Now it springs up; do you not perceive it?' (Isaiah 43:19). Faithfully serve. Commit your ways to me."*

To which I responded in complete annoyance:

"Well, now I'm discouraged...How am I supposed to handle this? I don't want to just 'trust,' I want something to change."

And God said, *"If you trust me, it will."* He reminded me of Psalm 37:5-6, which states, "Commit your way to the LORD; trust in him and he will do this: He will make your righteous reward shine like the dawn, your vindication like the noonday sun."

God was speaking to me, guiding my steps, advising my decisions, answering my prayers for help and direction, but I wasn't *listening*. When I look at situations like this with hindsight as my magnifying glass, I'm embarrassed by my lack of faith in God's promises and my failure to remember what He had told me. I also realized that my negligence in listening to the Lord wasn't always because I hadn't remembered what He told me, but because I wanted Him to tell me something new. Instead of listening to God, I wanted a new revelation to finally bring the rescue I desired.

As I reflect on this journal entry, it frustrates me that I had this conversation with the Lord *prior* to directing Royal Family KIDS Camp and *before* I was teaching first grade—both inspiring responsibilities that entirely broke my fervor. I wonder if I had just *listened* to God's wisdom and trusted in His promises, would my spirit have been strengthened to manage the weight of purpose in my life? I know that the emotional struggles I've faced are significant problems, ones that have required much processing, healing, and support. Still, I can't help but consider how my faith could have positively influenced the distress I felt.

In retrospect, I'm disappointed in myself for not carrying my responsibilities better, for not believing God was in control, for feeling distraught and defeated while leading and making a difference in children's lives, for not being *perfect*. Yet, I must accept the fact that I will never *be* perfect. God created me with intention and purpose, but that doesn't eliminate the flawed, human qualities of being myself. In my insecurities and inadequacy, I should not ridicule myself for my shortcomings but reach out to Christ to help me through my problems. In the grand scheme of God's plan for my life, it doesn't matter that I failed in my humanness to listen to His wisdom. What matters most is that I obeyed His will through the trials, learned valuable life lessons, and gave Him the ultimate glory for my life's purpose. Bringing us closer to Jesus, that's what matters.

During the years of trials and tribulations, I wasn't an example of what a "perfect" Christian should be, one filled with peace, faith, and holiness. I was simply the flawed human that I am, trying to follow God's will and fulfill His plan for my life. Second Timothy 2:13 says, "if we are faithless, he remains faithful…" Despite my failures and disappointments in confidently trusting the Lord, He will *always* be faithful. God is truly a *good* God, and He cannot be something that He's not—unjust, unfaithful, or unloving. We might not always understand the Lord's timing or His lack of immediate relief from our adversities, but we can confidently trust that when we obey to the best of our abilities, He will meet our needs and bring *good* from our hardships. God is always working, always moving, always patiently waiting for us to accept His call to action to work in our lives for the glory of His divine purpose.

Chapter Eight

The Deliverance

"When they walk through the Valley of Weeping, it will become a place of refreshing springs. The autumn rains will clothe it with blessings."

Psalm 84:6 NLT

*D*epleted. *Empty. Devoid. Dead.* That's how I felt while walking along the curved sidewalk toward the church's main entrance on that September morning in 2021. I had debated whether to attend the Women's Conference that year because I was so tired, yet here I was, strolling toward the doorway of the bustling lobby filled with hundreds of women gabbing, laughing, and praying together.

I braced myself for the social interactions looming upon entering the conference, feeling a physical daze in my spirit. It was an unusual feeling, like being a tangible, walking, talking, smiling, moving body, yet like I had no soul to feel emotions of love, hope, or excitement. While I participated during worship, singing each song filled with hope and promise, I lifted my hands toward heaven and yearned for their authenticity and truth. I wasn't worshiping in adoration of the majestic God I serve; I was crying out in desperation for rescue, hoping with all my heart that these lyrics weren't simply words written for entertainment but that they were the miraculous cure that would make my spirit whole again.

Back in August, I had tried to savor my last two weeks of summer break, attempting to take a respite from RFKC duties before the new school year began. I journaled my weariness to the Lord several times, explaining:

> *"I feel burnt out already. I'm so frustrated. I feel like giving up because I just can't maintain a 'win,' and my soul feels so defeated. I'm weary and exhausted. Lord, are things going to change?"*

> *"It's like my spirit is struggling to breathe. I'm exhausted and I refuse to do anything I don't have to in order to*

survive. I don't know what to do, where to go, how to feel better. Lord, will you help me?"

"I feel like my soul is dead, even though I'm well alive and not depressed. It's a very frustrating state to be in…It feels like I've lost part of myself, even though I'm well alive. I don't know what to do…"

Helplessness and hopelessness consumed me. I felt defeated, like there was no solution to redeem my zombified self. I cried out to God in desperation for relief, yet no matter how much I demanded rescue, God let me sit in that hollow shell of misery. As the days turned into weeks and the weeks turned into months, I doubted whether God would be faithful to meet my needs and answer my cries for help.

As fall approached, I was apprehensive about some changes happening at my school. The administration team had decided to pioneer a new extensive math curriculum under the leadership of a brand-new elementary principal, plus my roster of students was going to be slightly larger. It felt like an enormous elephant of stress had plopped down onto the delicate cushions of my anxious heart, the weight of responsibility practically suffocating me. Learning a new comprehensive curriculum, building a rapport with a new principal, and teaching additional students were more than I could manage in my emotional state. I didn't know how I would survive the pressure of the new school year.

During the first few weeks of school, I journaled my distress to the Lord:

"This school year has started in such chaos and stress; I can't imagine how draining this year will be. I don't know what to do about my weary spirit. I'm so tired and disappointed in myself..."

"...I feel like this 'season' just keeps getting harder and harder. Every day I go to work, there's one more thing on my plate or another dramatic issue. I don't want to go to work anymore...I know that I need to be positive, I need to believe, trust, and have faith. But I'm so tired, exhausted, and weary. I feel so defeated all the time about almost everything in life. Jesus, rescue me..."

"It's like my spirit is struggling to breathe..."

It was frustrating to feel like all I needed was time to renew my broken spirit and find my purpose in teaching again. Yet, the responsibilities of the new school year weren't going to allow that to happen. Being a teacher had brought me such joy and satisfaction, but now I was too exhausted to feel anything. I worried that if I didn't recover from the emotional turmoil soon, I could lose my passion for education altogether. I believed that God had created me to become a teacher, and that role meant everything to me; it was my *identity*. What would happen if I lost connection to my life's very purpose?

Being an educator is an exhilarating, inspiring, and exhausting profession. You are like a superhero to your students, tackling each question with a confident answer, defeating every dilemma with painstaking patience, training each student to learn the power of respect and responsibility, handling every situation with supernatural care. The art of teaching is similar to performing several different roles simultaneously within the same show—portraying the knowledgeable professor of all things academia, transitioning to the medically trained nurse of minor cuts and stomach pains, posing as the licensed counselor for all social conflicts, acting as the extraordinary entertainer of whimsical engagement, and improvising as the inspiring motivational speaker.

Despite my love for the job, the emotional stamina the role required felt impossible in my distressed state. I wanted to be the superhero my students deserved, to exude perseverance, invincibility, and inspiration in every teaching performance. I doubted my level of endurance, but I was committed to putting on my superhero disguise and trying to be the best teacher possible for my new batch of first-grade explorers.

My biggest concern was having the emotional capability to support my students. Quarantine and the social restrictions of the pandemic negatively impacted young children's social and emotional development, causing this group particular difficulty. The previous school year, the kindergarten teachers looked worn out every day after teaching their classes. I worried that if they had struggled to meet the needs of these students, how was I going to support them in my jaded state? I knew my class would be full of *good* kids—fun, loving, and lively little humans. However, as with any group of differing personalities and diverse learning abilities, my new explorers were going to require extra social and emotional support, requiring me to exude every ounce of positive energy I could muster.

It's not that a larger class size was the crux of the problem, especially since my roster only increased by four students. The major issue was this group's lack of self-control. Even during my years teaching preschool, I never encountered such a loud, chatty, and restless group of students! I had to constantly pull out all the stops to redirect behavior, especially during instruction. It never mattered how engaging I tried to make a lesson, whether I had students come up to the Smart Board for an activity or use their dry-erase boards to answer questions. Even when I planned a partner game or danced and sang my way throughout the classroom, they would find something to distract themselves or simply talk over me while I taught. I'd implement breaks to release their energy, ask questions to check for understanding, and use call-and-response techniques to give them an appropriate opportunity to shout out, but those efforts rarely seemed to make a difference.

It was physically exhausting and emotionally draining trying to engage my class and correct their behaviors simultaneously. I just didn't have the patience for their constant disruptions and lack of focus. In my weariness, I resorted to the easiest strategy I knew to maintain control: raising my voice. I never intended to yell at my students, although on some days I impulsively did. I knew there was a difference between raising my voice for attention and yelling in frustration, and I didn't want my explorers caught in the crosshairs of my irritation like I had been as a child during my parents' fighting. Yet, I struggled to contain my impatience.

When my students didn't listen, especially during an important lesson, I didn't know how to control my frustration. My signature expressions of displeasure were a loud holler of *"Excuse me?!"* or *"I'll wait!"* across the classroom as I stared until I had their undivided attention. This wasn't how I wanted to interact with my explorers. I wanted to be so much better—patient, understanding, and compassionate—especially since they needed that for the success of their first-grade year.

My reaction to raising my voice was probably more instinctual than a learned behavior, but I still didn't want to copy the negative habits of my past. I just didn't know what else to do.

The conflict between my depleted spirit and my desire to be a good teacher was endless. I didn't understand how God had gifted me to be a passionate educator, yet this year I struggled to support student behavior, created an environment of frustration instead of security, and failed to teach effectively. I believed that being a teacher was my ultimate purpose in life, and if I couldn't excel at that, then what was my value even worth? In my discouragement, I started to question my identity.

⊷—• •—⊶

A new planning season for RFKC began in mid-September. After finally leading our first in-person camp that summer, Jon and I knew the figurative and literal blood, sweat, and tears required for a successful week at camp. The stress we experienced while directing and working full-time was something we couldn't ignore, and Jon and I began having difficult conversations about our roles as directors. It was clear to us that I needed to restore my broken spirit because I could barely function (let alone lead). Unfortunately, Jon would soon be required to travel every other week for work while knee-deep in his last year of graduate school, restricting his spare time even more. As we evaluated our situation, we couldn't believe we were discussing stepping away from directing. *How could we possibly consider not being a part of RFKC?*

As we prayed for guidance, God graced our hearts with astonishing peace, letting us know that this was our time to step down as camp directors. We were devoted to RFKC, but we knew we weren't equipped to continue leading the ministry effectively. Jon and I agreed that the Lord was leading us toward a path of healing, and we obediently followed His direction.

After discussing our decision with our mentoring directors, I journaled this entry:

"...it feels like a weight has been lifted. We feel peace in knowing this challenging season is coming to an end, that we're headed into a season of healing and restoration which will prepare us for the next chapter God has planned. Our souls are grieved...But, there's no denying we are spent, burned out, and cannot take on the load of responsibility..."

When we met with the missions pastor of our church, she agreed that stepping down from leadership was the best solution for our personal circumstances. She gave us her full support and the church's blessing as she prayed for us with tears in her eyes, encouraging us to follow the Lord's will. As we left our leadership responsibilities to the church, we hung our director hats upon the hooks of faith, trust, and hope. We let go of RFKC and let God lead the ministry into a new future without us.

Making this decision was extremely bittersweet. Jon and I had peace in our hearts, yet the disappointment we felt was miserable. Directing RFKC had been the most inspirational thing we had ever done, sacrificing everything within ourselves to lead well. We poured every ounce of energy into our roles, striving to support our volunteers as they exemplified the love of Christ in each camper's life. We believed God had called us to serve, and we did so diligently. Yet now He was allowing us to leave the ministry after only two years of obedience. This didn't make any sense in my perfectionistic, identity-driven mind. If this was part of our predestined purpose, why didn't God provide help with our overbearing responsibilities? Why was He letting us step away from leadership entirely? Jon and I may have been confused by the Lord's plan and timing, but the truth of the matter remained: God was giving us peace to leave the ministry. Just as Jon and I accepted directorship with the Lord's blessing, we were now walking away from our position by His merciful grace.

I couldn't help but feel relieved. It felt like God had finally seen my internal suffering and instead of expecting me to keep moving forward, He was giving me time to recover.[1] Naively, I assumed that healing would begin immediately. I needed to learn from the wisdom of Ecclesiastes 7:13 (NLT), which says, "Accept the way God does things, for who can straighten what he has made crooked?" God works in His own timing to accomplish the goals of His will. Even though I believed God had a recovery plan in place, I soon realized that it wasn't going to happen at my desired time. I had to trust that the Lord would bring restoration; I just needed to wait for it to happen.

Walking by faith, not by sight or my emotions, was much more challenging than I anticipated (2 Corinthians 5:7). Begrudgingly, I learned this valuable lesson: God is not a genie. He does not grant every request nor meet every desire instantaneously. Even though the Lord had a plan of recovery for my downcast spirit, His actions (or lack thereof) to bring relief were slow-paced. Even without the pressures of directing,

---

1. Like David's petition in Psalm 25:17 when he asks of the Lord, "Relieve the troubles of my heart and free me from my anguish."

I still felt a void. I didn't understand why I *still* had to sit in a pit of anxiety when I knew that restoration was the next phase of my journey. I journaled my frustration to the Lord:

"God, I'm so tired of feeling so stuck. I'm tired of asking you for guidance and to speak to us every single day for months. When will you lead [Jon and me] out of this season? It feels overbearing, and I don't know how much more we can learn before we just give up. Changes need to be made in our lives, and we want you to open the doors...I know you have a plan; I know you hear our cries and prayers; I believe there is a joyful season for us to walk through; I know that your timing is perfect. But God, we are beyond weary, extremely stressed with our lives, feeling hopeless and useless. We don't know where to go or what to do."

"I know that you are faithful. But, this season has made me so weary, I'm not trusting that we'll come out of it. Lord, forgive my unbelief. Help me to have faith and trust in your plan and timing."

Even in my hopelessness, I chose to remember the promise of Psalm 9:10, which says, "Those who know your name trust in you, for you, LORD, have never forsaken those who seek you." This scripture reminds me that as I trust the Lord to move in my life and continue to follow His will and accomplish His purpose, He will not forsake me in my time of distress. Even though having faith was extremely hard, I had to believe in the promises of God's Word to sustain me.

Despite my efforts to bring my best teacher self to the classroom, I stumbled through the remaining months of the school year. In the spring of 2022, I recorded these two entries about the challenges I was facing:

"The meeting [re: my student] lasted an hour, and I had a panic attack during my ten-minute lunch…"

"I cried hardcore for fifteen minutes on my way home yesterday…My class is SUCH a handful! I'm just heartbroken and at the end of my rope."

I was so discouraged by my lack of endurance. I just could not function. The endless demands of my job, partnered with the Lord's delayed relief, made me contemplate the reality of my situation. I journaled my feelings to the Lord:

"In the last few weeks, I've had several thoughts about leaving education…Should I even be a teacher anymore?! I am worn out…"

"…This feels like a terrible school year. I don't know if I can make it…"

"This is the first time in my life that I'm seriously and wholeheartedly considering leaving my career field. This year has taken its toll on me already…I need direction toward what I'm supposed to do. What purpose do you have

for me? I long to be passionate and fulfilled again...I want to have joy teaching [my students]. Lord, show me what to do and where to go...This year is miserable."

I never thought that I would consider not being a teacher. The position I held (teaching first grade at a private Christian school) was supposed to be my dream job, an accomplishment that I believed was the essence of my identity as an educator. Yet, I couldn't deny the misery and inadequacy I felt. I knew the option to work at another school would not resolve my desperate need for a reprieve, so I figured the only solution was to leave my career entirely (at least for the time it took to recover and develop emotionally healthy and sustainable practices). As I tossed this idea to-and-fro in the corners of my mind, I was perplexed. I thought: *Who would I even be if I wasn't a teacher?* I had formed my identity around my role as an educator. How could I just walk away from God's calling on my life? However preposterous the thought seemed, it was something I contemplated for months as I struggled to survive the present school year.

Finally, the last week of school arrived! I expressed my relief to the Lord, journaling:

"I can't believe I've just about survived all of the chaos. I wish I had been a better teacher, but I gave all I could in my human strength. I don't know what kind of difference I made, but I pray that whatever seeds were planted in [my students'] hearts, you will use in their lives..."

I felt like I had spent the entire year wrapped up in so much angst that I wanted to spend these final days making positive memories with my explorers. A tradition I had with my class every year was a character award ceremony. I designated a jungle-themed certificate for each explorer and presented their awards individually in front of the class. At the end of that year's celebration, several students insisted on having another ceremony where *I* was the recipient of their specialized awards. It warmed my heart as students took turns trotting to the front of the classroom, demanding attention from their peers as they read aloud each certificate. However terrible I felt in my execution of being a mediocre teacher was briefly erased by the heartfelt sentiments of their thoughtful awards, each one mentioning affirmations like *good, kind, safe*, and *best friend*. My heart could've burst from the gratitude I felt hearing these generous comments from my explorers! Somehow, the Lord used my imperfect efforts to bring *good* into my students' lives that year (and in mine, too).

During the last few days of school, my plans of making fun-filled memories with my class were interrupted. My principal scheduled several meetings during my class time (instead of during my planning periods) to discuss curriculum changes for the next school year, requiring my teaching assistant to oversee the memory-making activities I wished to be a part of. I was genuinely disappointed to be missing this time with my students, and although these meetings were valuable, I left each one feeling even more overwhelmed.

After sitting through the last taxing meeting of the week, I returned to my classroom and sat at my desk, dazed by an unexplainable peace. I was beginning to feel a gentle nudge of courage confirming the reality I genuinely didn't want to be true: I was considering not returning to school in the fall.

When I got home from school that afternoon, Jon and I discussed the possibility of me leaving my dream career.

We scrutinized every doubt, fear, concern, hope, and desire that I had, updated my pros and cons list, and added notes of anything that might hinder my emotional recovery. After several hours of deliberation, I was finally ready to make the unbelievable decision not to return to the classroom the next school year.

The next morning, I wrote this journal entry:

"I made the decision last night to quit and not return to [school] in the fall...I felt peace, but I'm waking up with some nervousness... The unknown of fall and not having a job scares me, but I do know and believe that you'll provide. Lord, I don't want to do anything outside of your will. I have been trying to do what's right, even though I know I'm failing. God, you see my heart and know my deepest desires. Continue to lead and guide me...I can't believe I'm doing this!"

Although I felt at peace in my decision, I worried about having a job for the fall. It felt a bit irresponsible to leave my career and not know what I was going to do next. Would I find a new purpose to attach my identity to? Would I miss teaching and return to my life's passion? I couldn't see the light at the end of the tunnel, but I believed I was about to board the right train toward restoration.

During the last day of school, I treasured every moment—the last morning meeting, last snack-time prayer, last call-and-response for attention, last reminder to follow the rules, last partner activities, and last dismissal routine. This was potentially my last day with my last group of first-grade explorers, and I wanted to remember every second.

Twinges of fear poked at my sides as I thought about the conversation I would soon have with my superintendent. I knew that my choice to resign was necessary because I wasn't going to be equipped to do anything within (or even outside of) God's will until I was healthy and whole again. As I hugged each of my nineteen explorers goodbye, I was in great anticipation for what was about to happen.

As I walked to my superintendent's office, I prayed for the Lord's guidance during the impromptu meeting. Every stride I took was like gliding along a moving walkway of hope and elation, propelling me straight into a plump, leather chair in his office. While I sat across from my superintendent, I was surprised by my confidence in choosing to leave. I loved teaching, especially at this school. The reality of my decision plummeted into my gut like a rushing wave approaching the shoreline, then gently receding into the sea. My identity as a teacher, my partnership with this school, it was all ending.

My superintendent met my announcement with disappointment yet complete understanding and support. He prayed with me and kindly offered to have me back whenever I was ready to teach again. As I strolled away from his office, I couldn't contain the smile spreading across my face. A sense of pure happiness overcame every doubt about leaving my career. I was proud of myself for making that difficult decision and was grateful for the opportunity to simply let go and let God take full control.

After the meeting, I bounded toward my teaching partner's classroom to share the news. Stephanie and I had been first-grade teachers for the last three years and became close friends throughout the highs and lows of teaching.[2] Before long, we

---

2. Especially during the pandemic and the present school year. Stephanie and I *trauma-bonded*, if you will.

were each other's lifeline to survive each day in first grade. I was excited to tell Stephanie about my resignation because she was also taking a respite from teaching, and I knew she would support my decision and understand how I was feeling.

When I entered her classroom, I mouthed the words "I just quit" from across the room. Instantly, Stephanie got up to shut the door for privacy and asked for more details. As I explained the circumstances that led to my seemingly abrupt decision, Stephanie sat in complete astonishment and said, "I haven't seen you this happy all school year!" We spent several hours chatting about the stress we were leaving behind and the grief we felt not being first-grade teachers anymore. Gratitude consumed our conversation as we talked, each comment expressing appreciation to the Lord for placing us in each other's lives and for the privilege it was to watch God faithfully lead us both into new chapters of unexpected blessing.

My confidence after my resignation soon turned into suffocating fears of doubt and discouragement. Although I believed the Lord approved of my decision, I struggled to accept the reality of my choice. I was extremely disappointed in myself for not handling the years of trials and tribulations better, and I felt ashamed for not being able to carry the weight of responsibility the Lord had granted me while directing RFKC and teaching first grade. Walking away from my job felt irresponsible, even if only for a year. Leaving the career I worked so hard to achieve, a profession that brought joy and fulfillment to my life, was devastating. I persevered throughout my adulthood to accomplish goals and attain dreams I never knew were possible. I didn't understand why God needed to take those rewards away from me. Yet, it was obvious that God required full control of my life before I could experience complete healing. I wasn't going to find restoration by my own means; I had to trust in His timing, His purpose, and His strength alone.

In obedience, I tried to accept my fate and welcome the seemingly irresponsible season of wholeness. I spent the summer of 2022 acclimating to my new normal, establishing healthy practices and routines to renew my mind, body, and soul. Slowly, I began releasing the emotional turmoil that had overwhelmed me for so long, letting my entire being succumb to the soothing therapy of time and relaxation.

During this time, I began reading devotionals adjacent to my daily Bible readings, seeking wisdom and understanding as I analyzed the meaning of Scripture. One morning, I wrote this journal entry:

"My devotional talked about Matthew 9:17, the scripture about new wineskins.[3] It dawned on me that maybe to be prepared for a new season, before I burst and all was ruined, it was necessary for the success of this future season for me to move on and stop in order to preserve myself for what God has called me to next, something new and different. The skins and the wine are preserved because both are new together—my health and whatever God will call me to do will be new together."

I could see the metaphoric connection of the wineskins to my own soul. My internal health had endured intense

---

3. "And no one puts new wine into old wineskins. For the old skins would burst from the pressure, spilling the wine and ruining the skins. New wine is stored in new wineskins so that both are preserved." (Matthew 9:17 NLT)

emotional pressure throughout the last three years (probably my entire life, if I'm honest), and if I had remained where I was—depleted, depressed, and exhausted—I wouldn't have been prepared for what God had in store for my future. I believed that the Lord would use this moment of respite from my career to replace the wineskins of my heart, making my spirit strong, capable, and durable for my life's next purpose ahead. Only then would I be prepared for the outpouring of new wine. I didn't know what God had planned, but I knew that if He was taking such great lengths to bring restoration into my life, it was bound to be incredible.

⊰•— —•⊱

As I settled into a rhythm of rehabilitation, I sought the Lord for advice in determining what to do with my time. I needed a break to heal, but I also wanted to do something meaningful. That summer, I journaled an intimate idea to the Lord, saying:

> *"I've always wanted to write, and now that I have time, should I actually try? I have really enjoyed memoirs— would people read one about my life?"*

> *"I haven't stopped thinking about writing a memoir—is this your will to tell my story? Lead and guide me, Lord."*

The passion to share my life's story burned within my heart. I didn't know exactly where to begin, and I wasn't completely confident that people would want to read it, but something inside me told me to *try*. This spark of desire ignited in my soul, the warmth of its flame causing an excitement that I hadn't felt in a long time. I couldn't believe it, but I knew God was leading me to become an author!

In October 2022, I took the first steps toward making this book a reality. I spent several weeks going through old childhood mementos, reminiscing with old photographs, and rediscovering personal stories penned in past journal entries. I discovered a particular entry I had written when I was nineteen years old, which says:

> *"[A family member] said that she believes I'm to write a book about my life. I believe that's a word from [God]. I've always enjoyed writing and dreamed of writing a biography of sorts. I've been through a lot, and I wanna be a testimony to people."*

The reality of this entry hits me every time I reread it: *God put the desire to write a memoir in my heart thirteen years ago.*

Writing has always been something I enjoyed, but the idea of authoring and *publishing* my written work was something I never considered. I wrote to express myself, not for the entertainment of others. Realizing that God had used a family member to sow this inspiring seed into my heart at the onset of my adulthood journey was astonishing. And the fact that the Lord had preserved my passion for writing, cultivating the seed of inspiration throughout the years until it blossomed into this beautiful opportunity for me to share my testimony, was even more unbelievable. I felt entirely humbled by God's vigilant care. Despite all that I had experienced in life, He had this very plan to write my book already established. I had no idea of the relevance of my aspiration for journaling until this moment. Now, I could see the Lord's divine influence weaving this passion for writing throughout my life's story.

The truth of Ephesians 3:20 (NLT) resonated in my heart as it says, "Now all glory to God, who is able, through his mighty power at work within us, to accomplish infinitely more than we might ask or think." Every time that God directed my steps, reminded me of His promises, and helped me achieve my goals were moments of His mighty work within my life, and this book-writing venture was no different. The Lord was about to do immeasurably more than I ever thought possible through His predestined plan for me to write a *memoir*. Through the pages of this book, I began to discover the restoration I so longed to attain, a healing so intentional that it has completely changed my life.

As I wrote my memoir, I began the habit of self-reflection. I learned to look at myself and identify what made me who I am, discovering how my personality, past experiences, and learned behaviors have influenced my perceptions about life, myself, and my beliefs. Introspection is a *hard* practice, especially when you revisit damaging and shame-filled memories. But, looking at those instances and realizing they don't define who you are is quite liberating. The past might influence us, but it does not control our futures—unless we give it permission to. As I wrote my book and recognized that my emotional health was rooted in the trauma from my childhood, I realized that I needed to return to those places of grief, hurt, and resentment before restoration could occur in my life. The therapeutic healing of introspection has taught me the necessity of acknowledging my past, improving my mental health, and believing in God's faithfulness. Viewing my soul-recovery journey through a lens of acceptance instead of regret has helped me reframe my mindset, correct my anxious tendencies, and restore my passion for making a difference.

I've learned that there is not a circumstance so bleak, a problem too colossal, or a worry so trite that God will not bring something *good* out of it. When we are faithful, however imperfect we are, God will always honor our commitment to walk in obedience, and He will never withhold His hand of rescue or prosperity from us, even when we walk through the darkest valleys.

Fear is one implication of the mantle that I've battled from the beginning. It has been an old, shrewd adversary of my soul—fear of failure, fear of disappointment, fear of mistakes, fear of loss, fear of authority. Fear is an emotion that haunts my every move, creeps into every decision, and scares me to oblivion. It is also the reason for the overwhelming anxiety tied to my subconscious. Fear has been an ever-present source of destruction in my life.

After recently reading *The Lord is My Courage* by K.J. Ramsey, I began to understand the impact of my childhood trauma and the fear that caused the development of my anxious habits.[4] In her book, Ramsey explains:

> "Trauma tends to disrupt our body's path of return to the rhythm of rest. Even when the real danger has stopped, our nervous systems become acclimated to assessing risk. We get stuck in hypervigilance, subconsciously scanning everyone and everywhere for threats

---

4. K.J. Ramsey is a trauma-informed licensed professional counselor.

through our body's function of neuroreception. Our breath gets stuck there too."[5]

Ramsey defines fear as an absence of recognized safety, and while describing a fearful moment in her own life, Ramsey explains:

"I lived mostly stuck in states of stress all those years, not because I wasn't trying to trust God with my life but because there were so many cues of danger drowning me every single day...You get stressed and afraid not because you are bad at remembering Romans 8:28 or don't have enough faith over fear but because your body does not feel adequately safe." [6]

I realized that this was my reality. Due to the constant tension between my parents and the mantle's pressure of perfection, I developed an expectation of terror, subconsciously expecting danger to lurk around every corner. I tried to combat these fearful tendencies by striving toward perfection, hoping that my good efforts would influence peace and happiness around me. This was also a huge reason for my panic attacks, when anxiety physically caused my breath to catch inside my lungs and I lost all ability within myself to function. The influence fear has had in my life has been subtle yet powerful. It has silently crept into my very core, latching onto my soul with a fierce grip, strangling my self-esteem, and inhibiting my mind from finding peace and contentment.

---

5. K.J. Ramsey, *The Lord Is My Courage: Stepping through the Shadows of Fear toward the Voice of Love* (Grand Rapids: Zondervan, 2022), 253.
6. Ramsey, *The Lord is My Courage*, 29.

In her God-given wisdom, Ramsey encourages her readers to understand that courage amidst anxiety is the act of believing that God will hold us and love our troubled souls no matter what happens.[7] Although we will never completely escape the physical twinges of fear within our souls, we can find solace in knowing that we are held safely in God's protective love and that He will always walk alongside us.

In the fall of 2022, I began to understand the concept of danger awareness and perceived safety in my life. I journaled my conversation with Jon, explaining:

"Last night, I talked to Jon about how I'm feeling walking through this season of rest and no responsibilities...I mentioned how I used to be so motivated in life—don't snooze the alarm, get the to-do list done and feel accomplished, not satisfied being lazy, going through hard things and fighting to work hard and do well. This season feels so out of character because I feel such satisfaction, contentment, and peace in this slow pace of life. Jon said maybe it's because I've never been nor felt truly comfortable and safe in my environment before."

It was astonishing to recognize that it had taken thirty years for me to feel true safety in my physical world. I had masked my fear of danger by constantly going, moving, doing, and being that this time of healing was finally relieving my heightened nerves. I think part of feeling safe in life is about letting down your guard and trusting in the security of your environment. People are a huge factor in creating emotional safety, and it's impossible to feel secure when you're not properly loved, appreciated,

---

7. Ramsey, *The Lord is My Courage*, 169.

or supported. Even when we do have positive relationships, it's hard to accept their kindness when we've functioned in fear for so long. We don't know who or how to trust, leaving our guard up, anticipating danger at any moment. Before my marriage, I had safe relationships with family and friends, but I never let go of my fearful suspicions enough to experience complete security. When we learn to correct our fears and rest in the safety of comforting relationships, we release the terror in our hearts and trust that we will be protected. It was a sad realization knowing that I never let myself feel truly safe until now, but I'm grateful to have finally found security in my life with my husband. Now, I'm experiencing the wholesome environment I always wanted to create for my students, a place where I am safe, loved, and cared for unconditionally.

Although I've discovered true safety, that hasn't entirely eliminated fear from my life. My struggles with anxiety, doubt, worry, and depression are still there, waiting for me to regress and succumb to their overbearing pressure. The fear from the mantle of not being good enough might always be in the back of my mind, on stand-by for any moment that it can latch back onto my self-esteem and degrade my value. Yet, because of the security I have found, I now have the confidence to face my fears and rely on the Lord's mercy to see me through. Even when I fail to have perfect faith amidst fear, I can rest in God's grace and accept my faithlessness for what it is: imperfect humanness seeking protection from harm. The beauty of accepting every facet of salvation is that Jesus chooses to love us despite our imperfect faith, and He graciously prepares a safe place for us to rest, revive, and trust in His mighty protection.

During my soul-recovery journey, I began a quest to find my identity. I felt a bit lost not having a life goal to work towards, no career or ministry role to velcro my worth onto. Sure, I began writing my memoir, but that wasn't a lifetime calling. I needed to know that my life was still important, that I really was created for a reason. If I believed the promises in Scripture that say God created me with a purpose (Jeremiah 1:5), He made me with intention (Psalm 139:13-14), and my destiny was uniquely planned by God Himself (Ephesians 2:10), then there *must* be value in my existence. I began seeking the Lord for an answer, reading the Bible, and examining my life experiences to understand why I was created. If my sole purpose wasn't in my accomplishments, titles, or people's approval, then where was my identity supposed to be found?

In November 2022, I journaled this revelation to the Lord, explaining:

"I'm also realizing how you've stripped me of all that I am to bring me into this season that I've craved. You removed active ministry and the pressure and distraction it caused; you took away my career—my current dream job—and eliminated the purpose and identity I found in being a teacher...You've stripped me of anything I had to do in life that I found identity in, in order for me to become completely free...I had to let go to let God [move], and my desires of rest have been fulfilled...How freeing it has been to leave everything I held as purpose and fall into [God's] hands to find true purpose in His faithfulness."

Like an epiphany, I saw a glimpse of God's plan for my life, the details of my past imperfectly aligning to guide me toward this future moment. If it weren't for all that I had gone through, from the instability of my childhood to the emotional years of the trials and tribulations, I wouldn't be here, presently healing from the wounds of my past, standing in the grace of Christ without relying on anything or anyone else. I don't believe that God destined the negative, abusive, and soul-crushing things that happened in my life, but I do believe that He transformed those situations to bring goodness into my future. If I had not followed the Lord's will, found my passion for working with children, became a teacher, led Royal Family KIDS Camp, or begun this introspective writing journey, I wouldn't be in this moment, discovering my life's worth through the beauty of my salvation. Every step of my life's path, God has held me, protected me, and led me along His predestined plan for my existence. In Christ alone, my hope (and identity) is truly found.

My understanding of this revelation grew even deeper after attending a women's event in May 2023. The special speaker shared from Romans 8:28-29. The scripture states:

> "And we know that God causes everything to work together for the good of those who love God and are called according to his purpose for them. For God knew his people in advance, and he chose them to become like his Son..." (NLT)

From her sermon, I learned that God uses our pain to form us into the image of Christ—His one and only Son. She reminded us that the Lord will always be faithful to work things together for our good and deliver us from our trials, but we must understand the transformation that takes place before our rescue happens. This was a perspective I had never considered before. As a Christian, I knew that Jesus is the ultimate example for believers to imitate as faithful Christ followers, but I hadn't connected the significance of becoming like Christ through hardships.

Jesus was God incarnate. He was the only perfect human ever to walk this earth. During His ministry, Jesus encountered similar adversities that we've all experienced because He was human just like us. Christ felt the physical pain of stress and misery. He experienced the very real emotions of humiliation, ridicule, and discouragement. Because He was human, Jesus knew what it was like to live in a broken world, endure challenges, not want to do something even when it's expected of you, and cry out for desperate rescue. While Jesus prayed in the Garden of Gethsemane before His crucifixion, Luke 22:44 (NLT) says, "He prayed more fervently, and he was in such agony of spirit that his sweat fell to the ground like great drops of blood." The pressure of Christ's purpose about to be actualized was a physical burden, causing a medical condition known as hematidrosis to inflict His body.[8] Even when He was about to sacrifice His life for the atonement of all humanity, a purpose He already knew He would have to fulfill, Jesus appealed to God for reconsideration, saying in Luke 22:42, "Father, if you are willing, take this cup from me; yet not my will, but yours be done."

When I look to Jesus as my role model, I remember it's okay to accept my humanness. I can be confident in who God created me to be, not by excusing my shortcomings or mistakes, but by living full of grace, love, humility, and faith. Jesus was perfect because He is the Son of God. I'm human, and God

---

8. Rupturing blood vessels in the sweat glands.

doesn't expect perfection from me. Christ came to earth in human likeness to personify how to live in communion with God while also acknowledging our need for His redemptive power. I've discovered that the example Jesus set is not meant to condemn our imperfect actions but to encourage us to exemplify His love toward others and dedicatedly walk hand-in-hand with the Lord to fulfill His will in our lives.

As I dove deeper into the value of my identity in Christ, I realized God truly holds all the answers to my problems and He is faithful to meet me in my circumstances according to His perfect will. Although I've doubted the Lord's timing, I am now confident that even in the confusion and heartbreak of the most seemingly detrimental situations, His ways are always better than my solutions, and His timing is always better than mine. I believe the Lord uses every negative experience to help refine our perspectives of His love, grace, mercy, and faithfulness so that we can live free from fear, inadequacy, and perfectionism.

In Psalm 18:19, David boldly states, "...he rescued me because he delighted in me." God loves us more than we can possibly comprehend! He chose us, created us, and destined our lives to be blessed and full of good. I believe that when we accept salvation and choose to build a relationship with Christ, God delights in us. When we pray with an honest and thankful heart and spend time in praise, worship, and reading the Bible, we bring joy to our Father in heaven. God loves spending time with us, watching us develop our faith, and hearing our adoration of His goodness in our lives. God delights in knowing us.

When I reflect on the valleys the Lord has graciously walked me through, I am astounded by the transformation that has altered my perspectives and healed my brokenness. First Peter 5:10 says, "And the God of all grace, who called you to his eternal glory in Christ, after you have suffered a little while, will himself restore you and make you strong, firm and steadfast." This scripture represents where I am right now; this is my moment of restoration and strength upon a firm foundation of healing and recovery. As I close my eyes and evaluate my emotional health, I am pleasantly surprised by my reaction; I feel *better*. After years of grasping at perfection, living in gut-wrenching fear of pretty much everything, overcoming countless roadblocks, accomplishing unimaginable wins, and battling wars of inner turmoil, I am finally becoming *free*.

Writing this book hasn't been easy, and the emotions attached to each chapter's message have been paralyzing to process at times. But the goodness God has brought into my life through the therapeutic healing of writing this memoir has been unbelievable. I am humbled, honored, and profusely grateful for the restorative experience this book-writing journey has given me. Although I'm not sure if the mantle's lasting effects will ever completely leave my subconscious, I am confident that as I continue to self-reflect and face my fears, the Lord will help me overcome my insecurities. The more I choose to face the burdens of the mantle, the less power it has over my life.

Now, when I face stressful, depressing, or challenging circumstances, I am learning to release my attempt to control and cast my cares onto the compassionate shoulders of my Savior. In those moments of worry and fear, I practice breathing through the emotional pain of the situation, accepting the waves of chaos for what they are—simply waves—and choose to direct my focus onto the shore of resolution, relying on God's faithfulness to move forward and get me there safely. Although these frustrating patterns can be never-ending battles to conquer, I choose to believe that I am held safely in His compassionate love. As I rely on the truth of the gospel and believe in the promises of God, I am confident that each setback is not the end. I no longer hope for something *good*; I believe it will happen. And I choose to rest in the simplicity of that truth.

Processing our sufferings, however big or small they are, is not a fun thing to do. But I believe the more we reflect on our difficulties and understand how our emotional intellect works, we improve ourselves to become more like Christ and receive His redemption of our most sacred wounds. When we can accept ourselves and the lives we've lived as they are—precious yet broken, meaningful yet disappointing, exhilarating yet frustrating, lovely yet flawed—we find comfort in the Lord's unconditional love that wipes our every tear, clears our every transgression, and removes our every burden. Jesus proclaimed this truth in John 8:36, saying, "So if the Son sets you free, you will be free indeed." True freedom is found in a personal relationship with Christ. When we accept salvation and begin unpacking the baggage of life's most oppressive catastrophes, we place our control, self-worth, and the very essence of our being in the mighty hands of our Creator, the One who redeems every ounce of our suffering and positively changes the trajectory of our future for His glory and our prosperity.

Final Thoughts

I believe everyone has a story to share, and I hope that through my story, you can see the significance of your own. Our backgrounds may differ, our life struggles might contrast, and our beliefs may not be the same, but this one fact remains: we all have important stories to tell. No matter what you've faced in life—blessing or curse, prosperity or poverty, love or abuse—someone needs to hear your testimony. I believe that the struggles we experience in life can either entangle our potential or empower our testimonies. When we choose to face our fears and process our pasts, the stories of our resilience have the power to influence someone else's life for *good*. When people can relate, empathize, and rejoice in the sincerity of another person's story, they are given the opportunity to realize this simple truth: *they're not alone.*

It takes courage to be vulnerable and share your story. Discovering that the focal point of my story isn't on *me* but on the One who rescued me has been a source of fortitude to tell my testimony. The more I understand about myself—my quirks, my trauma, my purpose—the more I see God's fingerprint throughout my life. To me, telling your story isn't about validating your feelings or past hardships; it's meant to encourage others and showcase the Lord's work in your life. Acclaimed writer C.S. Lewis phrased my feelings this way:

"Don't shine so others can see you. Shine so that through you, others can see Him."

Completing my memoir has been an unbelievable experience, processing all that my life's story represents—trauma to healing, insecurity to confidence, brokenness to restoration, imperfect to (still) imperfect. I'm reminded of the truth in Psalm 40:2-3: "He lifted me out of the slimy pit, out of the mud and mire; he set my feet on a rock and gave me a firm place to stand. He put a new song in my mouth, a hymn of praise to our God. Many will see and fear the LORD and put their trust in him." It took me many years to process the mud and mire of my childhood trauma, to heal from the effects of such a slimy pit of anxiety. The effects from the mantle have been the hardest to suppress, the implications of fear, perfection, and doubt distracting my efforts toward complete restoration.

Yet, as I refuse to believe the lies of the mantle's expectations, I must consciously choose to trust in the stability of my faith in Christ. I know that no matter what I do in this life, how epically I fail or marvelously I achieve, I am worthy, valued, accepted, and loved. As I continue to recognize the mantle's legacy and work to diminish its influence in my life, a new song of praise forms in my heart for the redemption of my life's identity.

I'm grateful that my imperfect humanness does not define who I am nor the purpose for which God intended for my life. When I identify with the trueness of who I am in Christ—more than a conqueror (Romans 8:37), fearfully and wonderfully made (Psalm 139:14), a new creation (2 Corinthians 5:17), a child of God (John 1:12), beloved (John 3:16), and chosen (1 Peter 2:9)—I leave space for the Lord to renew my spirit and disprove any previous idea that my life's value was ever rooted in my past sufferings. Finding your identity in Christ means embracing who He is, how He loves you, and what He thinks about you. As the Lord restores our brokenness, He will gently guide us toward healing, leading us to the mountain peak of rejuvenation. Yes, it takes excruciating work, but just think, won't the therapeutic view of renewal be worth it?

While I reflect on the chapters of my life's journey (figuratively and literally), the chorus of this rendition of the classic hymn *Amazing Grace* serenades my heart:

"My chains are gone, I've been set free,
My God, my Savior has ransomed me.
And like a flood, His mercy reigns.
Unending love, amazing grace."[1]

The promise of deliverance in these lyrics brings me peace as I accept God's care in my life. It is by His unending love and amazing grace that I have discovered who I am and who I was created to be. My past troubles cannot define my worth and value. When we release our anxieties to the Lord—anything that chains us to the unworthiness we feel in receiving redemption—we put our lives, our very souls, in a vulnerable place of deep healing.

A friend recently told me that her parents were surprised when they heard I was writing a memoir. Apparently, they couldn't believe I had enough life experience at my age to be

---

1. Chris Tomlin, *Amazing Grace (My Chains Are Gone)*. Album. Six Step Records, 2006.

able to write an entire book! I paused to consider the comment, shaking my head as I thought about all the hardships I've faced in my thirty-two years of life—the verbal abuse, emotional trauma, academic struggles, testing roadblocks, responsibility overload, panic attacks, faltering self-esteem, and mental anxieties. As I reflected, I began to smile at the realization of all the *good* that has happened despite those adversities—my loving marriage, my successful teaching career, my supportive friendships, my positive impact for children in foster care, my improved physical health, and my emotional recovery. The woman I am today isn't who I used to be.

I am no longer the little girl who struggled with the mantle's perfection, nor the teenager who contemplated her self-worth and identity, nor the college student swerving between unexplainable failures and unbelievable accomplishments, nor am I the young woman establishing her career and finding her purpose in life's hectic pace of survival mode. I am now simply *me*, the person God created me to become from the very beginning—worthy, confident, capable, and restored. It is because of Christ that my life has been *redeemed*.

"My flesh and my heart may fail, but God is the strength of my heart and my portion forever."

PSALM 73:26

www.ingramcontent.com/pod-product-compliance
Lightning Source LLC
Chambersburg PA
CBHW020231130626

46549CB00005B/1831